THE ARCHITECTURE OF WINE

CLOS PEGASE WINERY

by RICHARD PAUL HINKLE

Design and art direction: Allan Green
Design and illustration: Victoria Hand

Global Interprint, Inc.
589 Mendocino Avenue
Santa Rosa, California 95401

Printed in Shenzhen, China

D DEDICATION

To Mitsuko, my wife and teacher, who initiated and encouraged me in the exciting and challenging odyssey of the fruit of the vine. *– Jan Shrem*

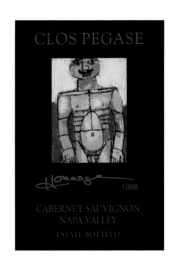

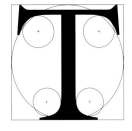

TABLE OF CONTENTS

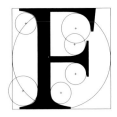

FOREWORD: WINE'S PROMISED LAND

By Jan Shrem

"Wine that maketh glad the heart of man." *Psalms 104: 15*

Over twenty years ago I sold a publishing business I built for twenty-five years in Japan and France so that I could make wine; I could have bought a small chateau in Bordeaux; or settled in golden Tuscany. I could have gone to New Zealand's pristine frontier. I had a dozen other alternatives. But I chose California's Napa Valley to plant vineyards even though I could have bought land in Mendocino County for one tenth the price I paid here.

I did not go wrong, for Napa was indeed wine's promised land. On December 28, 2000, noted wine writer Robert Parker wrote: "At the conclusion of what is undoubtedly the most extraordinary decade that California wine has ever experienced, it is no exaggeration to say that California wine has come of age and can now rival or surpass the world's finest wines." And he adds: "At the top level California wines are among the most exciting in the world, with many producers possibly rewriting the definition of greatness for Cabernet Sauvignon, Chardonnay and Pinot Noir."

Nature and science have endowed California's vintners with an enviable set of circumstances.

To begin with, unlike France or other Northern countries, California is guaranteed the sun every summer without fail, with rain being almost non-existent at this time, and rare during harvest. And the Napa Valley has a variety of elements that, combined with the advance of science and global exchange of ideas and procedures, give it a marvelous edge for producing top quality wines. There are many reasons for this.

The Wappo Indians who inhabited the Napa Valley called it Napa because it meant in their language "land of plenty." I call it an enchanted valley, carpeted in grape vines, diverse yet intimate in scale, being one to five miles in width and thirty in length, bounded on both sides by mountains of dramatic beauty. The waters of San Francisco Bay arrive at its southernmost maritime gates in the cool Carneros ("The coldest winter I ever spent was a summer in San Francisco" supposedly wrote Mark Twain), and the northernmost town of Calistoga is cradled between the sheer walls of the Palisades at the foot of Mount St. Helena on the east and the forested Mayacamas Mountains on the west.

Jan Shrem savors the inaugural Clos Pegase Cabernet Sauvignon: made with the assistance of Andre Tchelistcheff, doyen of the resurgence of the Napa Valley in the 1970's and 1980's.

With the influence of these mountain ranges and the Pacific Ocean, in addition to San Francisco Bay's very deep body of cold water, the valley enjoys a temperate climate perfectly suited to the growing of fine wine grapes. A long growing season marked by sunny, warm days and cool evenings gives grape clusters a longer "hang time" for ripening slowly and evenly. With thirty different soil profiles of volcanic, maritime and alluvial origin, many distinct microclimates emerge.

While Europe culls from many centuries of experience and history, we have borrowed grape varieties and winemaking skills from them and we have added new rootstocks, clones and techniques, with much help from modern science and UC Davis. Experience has shown us the wisdom of matching rootstocks, clones, spacings and trellises to locations whose microclimates and soils are best suited to particular grape varieties.

Today, while retaining the European varietal origins, Napa Valley wines exhibit all of the exuberance of the new world, clearly expressing the terroirs of the region and the artistry of the winemakers. It is a memorial to all the events in the cycle of making wine with the participation of the grape growers, enologists, craftsmen and cellar rats. The story of their wine is told hanging from the twisted vine stock, locked up in dim cellars, resplendent in the transparency of the glass, painted about, sung about, admired and then tasted with all the enthusiasm that the promised land of Napa Valley inspires.

Aerial view to the southwest of the winery and residence soon after completion.

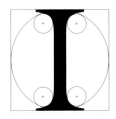# Introduction: Wine as Magic

"As far as we can discern, the sole purpose of human existence is to kindle a light in the darkness of mere being." – Carl Gustav Jung

You might not think it fair to ask a single wine to represent an entire winery, but I believe that the 2005 Mitsuko's Vineyard Pinot Noir is up to the task on all counts. I say that because it is a wine that raises the vinous ante from mere being—most wines are nothing more than fermented grape juice—to something special, something that adds light and character to the equation. Furthermore, this is a wine that exemplifies each of the elements that set Clos Pegase apart from other wineries, those elements that give Clos Pegase its personality, its marvelously singular identity.

In its entirety, this wine demonstrates how great wines are works of architecture, from ground to glass, that there is an intelligence—built upon personal and cultural experience—that is put to play from site selection to grape variety match-up, from vineyard practices to fermentation and aging regimes. You might think it a no-brainer to plant the Pinot in the Carneros, Napa's coolest (in terms of temperature and in terms of *chic*) appellation, but then you layer on the clonal selections—five Dijon clones and the heritage Pommard selection—and work them on a pair of clay-loam soil series,

and it gets just a tad bit more complicated. Since complicated, when handled artfully, leads to wine complexity, well, that counts as a good thing. A very good thing.

Harvested in the middle of September, the grapes were crushed and the juice fermented entirely with native yeasts, the better to elicit each clone's truest grape essences, put through malolactic to temper the region's raised natural acidity, then aged in slightly less than half new French oak barrels for nine months. Several months in bottle prior to release yielded a wine of concentrated fruit—strawberry, black cherry, plum and blueberry, with a hint of clove and black pepper spiciness, further nuanced by rose petal aromas—that is nonetheless fluid and succulent in texture, the best of what the variety is capable of. As winemaker Shaun Richardson suggests, "This wine has richness and intensity in the nose, yet retains great finesse and complexity on the palate. The palate is rounded, fleshy and opulent, with lush fruit and great length."

That is the great balancing act of wine as architecture. When it is done well, you find in the

The 2005 Pinot Noir joins the Chardonnay and Sauvignon Blanc in using the Stelvin screw top.

wine many layers of expression, and not all of them at once. The wine—like any great work of art—opens itself as a flower opens its petals, one layer of meaning here, another layer of expression there. Each time you come to the wine it reveals yet another iota of personality, yet another aspect of its character. That is the beauty of complexity, in wine as in art, that ever-changing revelation of essence, of spirit, of core quality. Beauty, in a word.

Beauty is the essence of all that Clos Pegase is, from its very name, on through the vineyards, the winery, the winery's accoutrements, and on to the wines themselves. The offspring of Poseidon and Medusa, Pegasus, as you surely recall from your many nights perusing Bullfinch's *Greek Mythology* or Robert Graves' *The Greek Myths*, was the winged stallion who, by striking the slope of Mt. Helicon with one of his sharp hooves, created the fountain of Hippocrene (the sacred Spring of the Muses). Hippocrene irrigated the vines that produced the wine that inspired the Muses who went on to create, among others, both beauty and art.

That, in a nutshell, is why Odilon Redon's classic interpretation of Pegasus graces the Clos

Pegase labels. "I believe that wine is an art form that deserves its place among the other sublime treasures of the art world," says Shrem. "That is why I chose, for our label, Redon's famous painting. Redon, as you know (ah, the charm of the man), was the foremost French symbolist of the nineteenth century, and was known as 'The Prince of the Dream.' Our winery 'temple' is *our dream*, our artistic rendition of the melding of art and wine. And that is the essence of Pegasus and the spring: It gave birth to art, and to wine."

Art and beauty are so important to Shrem that the works of a wide variety of other artists are employed for the winery's Hommage series of wines. Artists the winery has paid homage to—these are all works owned by Shrem—include Salvador Dali, Miro, Klee, Kandinsky and Jean Dubuffet.

When Shrem talks about wine, and the art and architecture of wine, the one thing that comes through with crystal clarity is his undiluted passion for it. "You know," he says with charming modesty, "I created this temple as much to share my passion as to fulfill the desire of others for

6

Odilon Redon (1840-1916),
Pegasus, c. 1890.

the knowledge which had become my culture. I wished to open the gates to my world to others. I wanted to reveal to the neophyte, as well as to the gourmet, the passer-by, the visitor with an inquiring mind, what goes on behind that little-known scene of the vineyard and the winery."

"Clos Pegase is a memorial to all the events in the cycle of making wine. It is a temple not only to pay homage to wine, but also to the men and women who love it and grow it—grape growers, enologists, craftsmen, cellar rats and poets. Clos Pegase is a book in which I have attempted to write not only my own biography and that of wine in general, but especially that of the Napa Valley."

The man is hardly above quoting others to support his position that wine is a multi-faceted benefit to mankind. He unabashedly points to Benjamin Franklin, who wrote, "Wine is…constant proof that God loves us and loves to see us happy." Franklin also noted that wine "makes daily living easier, less hurried, with fewer tensions and more tolerance." The last, of course, would be a great benefit, in and of itself, in the modern world. Then there was Thomas Jefferson, who counted "good

Left: Tony Smith (1912-1980) Marriage (Black Gate), 1961 at Applebone Vineyard.

Right: In homage to Henry Moore's passing in 1986, the year of the winery opening; Mother Earth (1957-1958) graces the entrance portico.

wine" a necessity of life and was a grape grower himself: "I have lived temperately...I double the doctor's recommendation of a glass of wine a day and even treble it with a friend." Jefferson considered making and promoting wine a service to his country: "By making this vine known to the public, I have rendered my country as great a service as if I had enabled it to pay back the national debt." Let us not forget the marvelous Sufi mystic-and-poet Jelaluddin Rumi: "When grapes turn to wine, they long for our ability to change."

Shrem's creation, on the south side of Calistoga, is clearly that synthesis of art and wine that he initially sought. The harmony of the two can be clearly felt as one enters the grounds, gracefully spotted with sculptural works as rooted and appropriate as to seem as if they had grown from the earth on their own. As you walk through the caves, the artworks that grace the walls equally exude a sense of belonging naturally to a place where liquid grape juice reposes, silently gathering itself in character and in personality.

At the end, Shrem has the artful ability to see wine in its most holistic sense, that wonderful process by which light and water are transformed—with all artistic senses—into that magical liquid that fortifies us and makes us more human. He is fond of quoting the noted wine writer, the eloquent Brit Hugh Johnson, on the many facets involved in growing grapes for wine: "The winemaker is both farmer and artist, drudging and dreaming, a hedonist and a masochist, an alchemist and an accountant." That, in a nutshell, is the art and architecture of wine. It is of the earth and it is of the heavens. It is part substance and part spirit. It is, in a word, magic. We are fortunate that that magic has a practical side. See, smell and taste for yourself.

Left: Cardenas (1927-2001) Memory of Dreams, 1972 at Applebone Vineyard.

THE COMPETITION: DESIGNING A WINERY

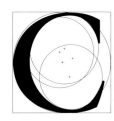

"Mind takes form in the city; and in turn, urban forms condition mind."
–Humanist architectural critic Lewis Mumford, The Culture of Cities

Mumford was talking about how architecture influences a place, "utilizing or denying the natural site" and recognizing the importance of "space." He also spoke of the necessity of "organic human purpose" to architecture. When Jan Shrem set out to seek a design for his new winery-to-be he seemed instinctively to recognize the importance of how this site, at the foot of a knoll, was going to be used. Could a winery be constructed in a manner that would honor the earth, yet take the wings of Pegasian creativity as well? The exercise would prove to be akin to walking a tightrope, and the early returns were heavily sprinkled with positives and negatives.

Shrem decided upon an international design competition as a means of putting a little pepper into the stew, putting new ideas to work. Above all, he wanted a construction that would seem to have grown out of the earth, aligned with the myth of Pegasus, yet seeming to be almost there of its own volition.

In one way, Shrem was not the first to look to the world of art and architecture for something unique and personal. Robert Mondavi had hired Cliff May in the mid 1960s to put a new face on Spanish ranch design for his Oakville *casa de vino*. Donn Chappellet gave winery architect Richard Keith a similarly free hand, which led to the vineyard pyramid that graces the family's vineland plot above Lake Hennessey, while Craig Roland got the nod for the similar cruciform (near-pyramid) shape that rises out of Rodney Strong Vineyards over the hill in Sonoma County. One must neither forget Tom Jordan's French chateau in Healdsburg—he was unable to buy one in France— nor the Aegean-inspired, mountaintop monastery look that the English founder of Sterling Vineyard brought to Calistoga.

In a lilting, almost laconic twist, Shrem had set up his dreamworks directly across the street from that English aerie. The further—and by far the more intriguing—twist came when Shrem, the wily Lebanese publisher, chose a competition as a way to prod and spark yet newer, yet more intriguing creative notions of wine facility design.

"We worked with Henry Hopkins, the director of San Francisco's Museum of Modern Art, to set up and sponsor the two-stage, open-design

The winning Michael Graves and Edward Schmidt model.

competition in 1984," recalls Shrem. "I wanted a beautiful place—neither Napa Valley barn, nor French chateau—in which Mitsuko and I could live and work, and display the many works of art we had collected over the years. Above all, we wanted the design to meld with the landscape, to marry art and winemaking. We wanted something practical, yet romantic."

Ninety-six architect-and-artist teams responded to the initial request for proposals. Of those, just ten were formally interviewed. Finally, five teams

were invited to enter the actual competition: Batey & Mack/Peter Saari; Robert Manguirian/James Turrell; Stanley Saitowitz/Toby Levy, Pat O'Brien and Elyn Zimmerman; Daniel Soloman, Ricardo Bofill, Patrick Dillon/artist Ed Carpenter and landscape architect Barbara Stauffacher Soloman; and Michael Graves/Edward "Ted" Schmidt.

Said Hopkins, "Our jury evaluated their designs based on the integration of art and architecture, especially architecture in relation to time and place—that sense of place that resulted

14

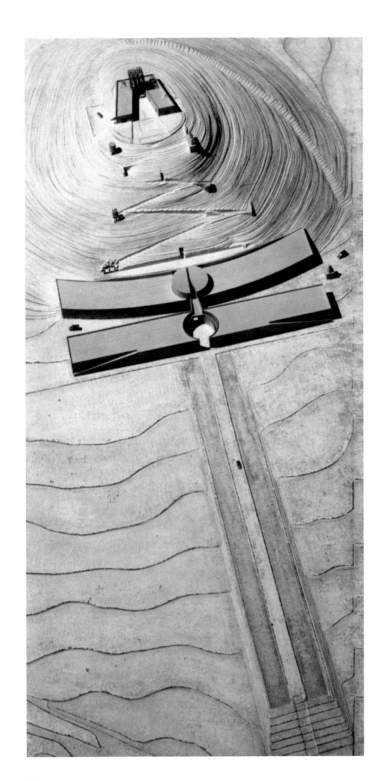

from the distribution of functions over the site." In the end the jury selected the postmodernist design of Harvard-educated, Princeton-based architect Michael Graves, and artist Ted Schmidt, whom Graves had met through the American Academy in Rome.

THE WINNING DESIGN

"We drew heavily on the Pegasus myth," said Graves, "both in the organization of the site

Architects Batey and Mack with artist Peter Saari.

Architects Daniel Soloman, Ricardo Bofill and Patrick Dillon with artist Ed Carpenter and landscape architect Barbara Stauffacher Soloman.

Architect Robert Manguirian with artist James Turrell.

and in the integration of the artwork with the architecture." Graves, now paralyzed from a viral infection, is known as one of the 'New York Five.' He designed the NCAA Hall of Champions in his hometown of Indianapolis, Indiana, supervised the expansion of The Whitney Museum in New York City, and designed the Public Library in the California mission town of San Juan Capistrano. He is also known for a domestic line of household items featured in Target stores nationwide.

The winning design was organized along an axis of water, beginning with the myth's spring, the grotto of Pegasus, carved into the summit of the knoll, the site of Shrem's private residence, and winding down to the winery's natural springs below. To the west of this axis are the open-to-the-public winery tasting room and the sculpture garden; to the east is the winemaking facility.

A dramatic circular, open-air pavilion at the base of the hill was intended to symbolize a mountain, and would have been ideal for wine tastings and parties. The interior was designed to feature a long, continuous frieze, a painting by Schmidt that was to depict the cycle of

winegrowing through the four seasons, from planting to harvesting, from winemaking to the enjoyment of the finished product. Sadly, none of those parts of the design—the aqueduct, the pavilion, the painting—were to be executed. Instead, a good portion of the winemaking process was later moved to an extensive system of caves dug into the base of the knoll. Caves, as you know, provide the constant temperature-humidity milieu that is ideal for the maturing of fine wines. They also allow a dramatic backdrop for the display of much of the Shrem's art collection.

In his competition statement, Graves commented on his attempt "to evoke memories of a European ancestry" by explaining "Character has been suggested by our attempt to establish a more archaic or timeless sensibility. Within the narrative or esthetic text of this setting, the stories of winemaking and habitation can best be told. We saw the waters of the Mount Helicon spring as providing both spiritual and physical sustenance, as the arts inspire our imagination and the waters irrigate our fields. It is fitting that Dionysus, god of wine, was the favorite pupil of the Muses, for

also within the art of winemaking there exists the duality of the process of making the wine and the pleasure of drinking it. Within this large context we have developed the themes of winemaking, the cycles of the day and the seasons, and the relationship of the man-made to the natural landscape."

THE JURY

Robert Mondavi was one of the members of the jury. When he crafted his Mission-styled winery in Oakville in 1966, it was the first new winery of any size built in the Napa Valley since the repeal of Prohibition. More than 95 percent of the wineries in the valley today were built after his.

Said Mondavi of the Graves presentation, "I am tremendously excited and inspired by this example of integrating some of the finest artistic talent available with an effective, producing winery. I believe this project will set the tone and pace for new winery developments to come."

As a whole, the jury found Graves' design "most appealing in the timeless quality of the site plan and its integration into the landscape.

It embodies a celebration of the lifestyle that is unique to the Napa Valley. The collaboration between artist and architect is classically blended into the design—art as architecture and architecture as art…The site development plan is a brilliant piece of work. It segregates public functions from private; recognizes service-vehicular functions as distinct requirements; creates opportunities for discovery, adventure, and invention; and has a poetic complexity that will age well."

That last half of the last line, I think, sums up what truly excited the jury about rewarding Graves and his project team (which included Terry Smith, Juliet Richardson, Ronald Berlin and Heidi Richardson). The notion of "discovery" and "adventure" are often lacking in designs that are so often dry and desultory. Add "poetic complexity" and you've got something that is going to survive the next flavor-of-the-month wine barn and become, over time, iconic in its own right. Wrote the French philosopher Henri Bergson, "*Je suis une chose qui dure*" (I am a thing that lasts). This is a thing that will last.

Michael Graves: South Elevation, 1984.

Left: Michael Graves, Winery Entry Portico Study, 1984.

Right: The classically 'Post-Modern' entrance portico blends into the landscape.

THE EXHIBITION

In 1985, the San Francisco Museum of Modern Art hosted an exhibition of the competition entries entitled "art + architecture + landscape, the Clos Pegase Design Competition." Concurrently, the Museum published a companion book of the same name, the drawings of which now reside in several private collections. The gouache painting of the mountain façade that Graves produced for the competition was turned into a limited edition print by printmaker John Nichols (New York City).

Later Graves' drawings—and the competition model itself—were featured in a nomadic international exhibition on the history of wineries in the late 1990s and in USDesign 1975-2000 (which began at the Denver Art Museum, then toured our country from 2002 to 2004). The winery itself received AIA New Jersey design awards in 1985 (as project) and 1987 (as built), and a National AIA Honor Award in 1990. In 1988 the Pompidou Center in Paris promoted an exhibition—clearly inspired by Shrem's competition—entitled "Chateau Bordeaux," an attempt to assess the artistic, historic and commercial roles of winery architecture in

that historic region. The exhibition was in three parts: Bordeaux chateaux, the Pegase competition, and a contest to design a hypothetical Bordeaux chateau of the future.

The Pompidou's director of architectural projects, Jean Dethier, who marveled at the Pegase design, finding great commonality between it and the Bordeaux model, made the following incisive comment at the time: "The Bordeaux region has created a veritable 'civilization of wine,' which is manifested by a relation, both traditional and privileged, between the quality of its wines and the richness of its architecture. Bordeaux, over the

centuries, invented the notion of the wine chateau, representing, as it does, not only the place where wine is made and aged, but also the prestigious symbol of the wines of the entire region."

Frank Prial, the noted *New York Times* wine critic, once cleverly compared the Pegase design "with the set for a DeMille spear-and-sandal epic." Yet it is clearly more than can be explained by mere quip alone. Design critic Martin Filler saw it as an expansion of design boundaries, writing, "Michael Graves is not just a very accomplished architect: He is a strong and extremely influential teacher, and there is a pronounced streak of the didactic

The essence of the Graves design was kept, although some features did not make it to the finished building.

The architecture of wine, melded into the landscape.

in his designs, which encourage us to experience things in just the way he wants us to, rather than being subject to the open-ended experience of most modernist architecture. Graves has points to make, and so does Jan Shrem. His conception of Clos Pegase as a place for enlightenment and inspiration has found a very clear echo in his architect's interpretation…in a world of increasingly narrowing artistic and architectural horizons it demonstrates that there are other great rewards indeed to be won by widening our field of vision."

Of the final product, opened to the public in May 1987, architecture writer Diana Ketcham suggests that Pegase "is an unapologetically classical building, not a replica but a suave

rethinking of Palladian portico and pediment, Tuscan columns, with proportions influenced by Ledoux, rendered in creamy stucco and crowned by a massive red tile roof. There is nothing like it among the flurry of arch experiments we call 'Postmodern Classicism.'"

Overall, the Mediterranean feel is both charming and complete. The entrance portico, supported by massive pillars, suggests permanence. The asymmetrical Tuscan tower, the chimneys, the intervening cypress and oak trees, as well as the earth tone coloring, allows the structures—including the Shrems' home, perched atop the wooded volcanic knoll—suggest an integration that is, again, charming and complete.

22

All of which speak directly to the inherent modesty, along with well-formed and exquisite taste, that the Shrems bring to the table. Or, in this case, to their little mountain. "Wine is an art form that should delight, illuminate and surprise," Jan likes to say. So too, as it turns out, is a winery.

THE WORKING WINERY

"There is neither a painting in the mind nor a mind in the painting: and yet, where else can one find a painting than in the mind?" – *Avatamsaka Sutra*

When you look at the final facility—the winery that was, in the entire practical sense, actually constructed and has since provided work to artisans, idealists and craftsmen alike—what you see remains something of a "painting in the mind." For this working place came out of the creative process, passing through the more artistic "theoretical" and on to the working "practical," all the while retaining that shining sense of the painting, that surreal vision of Pegasus at work in the real world. The muse at work; the muse actually *working*.

The most fascinating aspect about the winery, to me, is instantly evident to even the most casual viewer: the facility is so imbedded into its landscape that it nearly melds—maybe "morphs" is the better word—into the hillside it was built into. The colors of the winery—the burnt umber of red clay, the tan of sandstone—are the colors of the earth, and the buildings almost seamlessly thread themselves into this low, timbered foothill. In fact, the single, sturdy, rust-colored column supporting the entry to the main courtyard seems like a redwood tree, specially fitted to that space,

while the terra cotta tiles on the Greco-Roman building's roof might well be fall leaves destined for the "forest" floor of the surrounding foothill. An identical column stands at the other end of the entrance portico leading to the beautiful courtyard with 52 cypress trees and in front of them is a more than 300 year old oak tree that serves as a fulcrum to the Sculpture Garden. At the entryway, Henry Moore's 'Mother Earth' captures all of those sensations perfectly. Notice the three towers: one in the office wing, one before the chandeliered Harvest dining room, and one in the bottling room. Notice also that the courtyard separates the facility: the working area on one side and the hospitality/pleasure wings on the other, for the celebration of wine and its inherent sensuality— openly, gleefully and with great relish. Note that on this same side, the architect built the owners' home way above the knoll, "for celebration."

THE SCULPTURE GARDEN

Neither is it a stretch to suggest that traipsing the grounds is akin to walking through a working museum of art, from the pair of giant balanced ball

Considered the greatest sculptor of the 20th century, Henry Moore specialized in organic, biomorphic forms which imbue his work with humanism.

Opposite: The entrance portico.

sculptures, executed by Mitsuko, at the entry to the winery and parking lot, to the more mundane nature of crush pad and fermenting room, a soaring roof supported by just one giant beam. From the garden areas with their dazzling array of artistic impressions, to the dark entrance of the caves where a cathedral/theatre rises within, the artistic modality that infuses Clos Pegase is visible at every step and permeates in every way. Better, the zest and vigor and eclectic nature of the artistic sensibilities of Jan and Mitsuko infuse and inform everywhere.

Not far from Mitsuko's balanced balls, she naughtily designed a huge one on a short pedestal and a smaller one on a tall one, is a wild Dubuffet sculpture in red, white and blue. At the far side of the parking lot is Anthony Caro's yellow and red 'Sunshine.' British-born, Caro settled in Bennington, Vermont, and this steel sculpture speaks to the vibrant sunshine he found there (too easy a contrast to his native land, no doubt). Americans George Rickey ('Two Lines Up, Oblique') and Robert Morris ('Wheels II' and 'Barrier') and the British sculptor Richard Deacon (he prefers the title "fabricator") are nearby. As

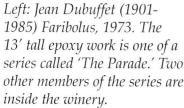

is the China-born American Mark Di Suvero's orange-red 'Applebone,' which sharply dominates the area, giving its name to one of three Clos Pegase Cabernet Sauvignon vineyards.

Perhaps the most viewed, most pondered-over piece in the Shrems' entire collection is Cesar Baldachini's more-than-six-foot-tall *'Pouce'* (thumb); this piece is number seven of an edition limited to eight and the only one in North America. It won a local newspaper's contest as "the most photographed object of the Napa Valley" and has a strange fascination for visitors. Some have chosen to marry by it.

"Cesar is known simply by his first name," says Jan. "He studied in the Beaux Arts schools of Marseille and Paris, but the path he chose took

him far from the classical canon of academic sculpture. Born in 1921, by 1965 he had acquired an international reputation for experimentation and sure and certain instinct for sculptural values. He is a witty fellow, and his pointed compositional eye has enabled him to produce a wide range of highly inventive figurative and abstract works that testify to both his versatility and his integrity." Shrem notes that the French equivalents to our Academy Awards are not called Oscars, but rather "Cesars." Not statuettes, they are rather pieces of gold that he compressed into rectangular cubes that are worn as pendants. Jan and Mitsuko are proud to own a pair of these golden pendants, gifts from the artist himself.

The Contemporary Sculpture Garden—the "enclosed place" the French word *clos* refers to—is one focal point of the couple's artistic journey. Immediately to the right as you step into the courtyard from the entrance portico is perhaps the proudest jewel of the Shrem's collection: The Torino Royal Bacchus. "Yes, we are most fond of this tri-color marble fountain," exudes Jan. "It comes from the Italian Royal Palace and features a depiction of Bacchus, the Roman god of wine. It is extraordinary for its richness of detail, and the Bacchus is set in a Renaissance niche and dome." "You know", he says with a wicked grin, "this lascivious Bacchus bears a striking resemblance to one of our former winemakers. They could have

been twins, separated at birth!"

Fifty-two cypress trees line the sides of the central walkway, symbolically intended by the architect to represent the 52 working weeks of the vine, and in the northeastern corner of the garden—adjacent to the grand old oak—is a magnificent 17th century patinated Renaissance bronze Florentine fountain that features four infant Bacchi under a Roman temple replica, four nymphs and four muses, with lions' heads spouting cool, clear water and dominating the restful picnic garden.

Contemplation is as good for the soul as wine and food are for the body; equally, the sustenance of soul and body are best taken not in haste

Opposite: The serene courtyard, reminding us of Grave's exceptional skills in spatial relations.

Left: Robert Morris (b.1931) Barrier, 1962.

Right: Robert Morris, Wheels II, 1963-1988. Morris's corten steel sculptures embody a single, relatively simple idea, composed of simple geometric forms.

Torino Royal Bacchus Fountain. One of the Shrem's most prized treasures, this 19th century tri-color fountain depicting Bacchus in Carrara marble graced the Italian Royal Palace.

but with deliberate measure. In fact, bring your picnic basket: the grass is green and comfy. "We want people to take their time and *feel* the many connections inherent in the mixing of wine and food and the arts," says Jan, that ever-present merry twinkle in his eyes. "Mitsuko decides all of the placements. She has a very good eye." An intentioned understatement, I warrant.

THE TASTING ROOM

The *Washington Post* called Clos Pegase "America's first monument to wine as art" since almost a thousand works of art are on display, including hundreds of sculptures, paintings, wine related antiquities and wine vessels. While showcasing a mind-expanding array of art—as does each of the winery's public rooms—the tasting room exudes a special pizzazz, both from the act of being able to taste the wines themselves, but also

from the energy and information that's available from the well-schooled hosts behind the counter. The well-chosen musical background—"Always classical when guests are here, but there's other music played when they're setting up," Jan admits with a knowing wink—further sets the mood for expanding one's understanding of wine as fluid creativity brought to life. He points to a large drawing of a Pegasus by Redon. "He did more than five hundred charcoals of horses…and every one of

them has wings!"

Pay close attention to the exact replica of Michelangelo's Bacchus that commands the middle of the main counter, made from a cast taken of the original found in the Florentine Bargello Museum. He decidedly looks like a fellow who enjoys his wine. Nor should you ignore the massive, marvelous mural that completely dominates the wall behind the counter of a Bacchic scene by the Renaissance artist Mantegna. "I do get more

A Bacchic mural by the Renaissance master Mantegna (1431-1506) gives an appropriate backdrop to the tasting room bar and tasting room manager Cherilyn Hays.

Karel Appel (1921-2006)
Personage, 1970.

sensual as I get older," says Shrem with a flash from his laughing eyes. "People who are drawn to wine are a different breed. I am so lucky to be in this business, I have made ten times more friends than in the publishing business since those attracted by wine are a different breed, always sensual." The ultimate salesman in him comes out when you see replicas of his art collection…for sale as refrigerator magnets. Ha!

In the small gallery next to the main tasting room—now dedicated to tasting the Pegase Reserve wines—are paintings by Lipschitz, Appel and the original Dubuffet Jan lovingly calls "The Full Monty" of the governmentally rejected 1988 Hommage label. That decision was eventually

reversed, with the 1998 *Hommage*, after many newspaper editorials condemned the BATF for art censorship.

Hanging precariously from the ceiling, dead center, is Michael Scranton's 'Wrecking Ball,' with a very frayed cable, looking full well as if with one swing it could bring down the ceiling on someone's head. Don't spread it around, but it is hollow, and weighs in at a mere 200 pounds. Scranton's Texas humor, no doubt.

Beyond the glass doors of the Tasting Room, amid the upright oak tanks, is a collection of ancient wine vessels spanning four thousand years.

THE HOSPITALITY WING

Opposite the offices, on the north side of the entryway, is the hospitality wing. The Shrems are gracious and easy hosts, and the grand 'Harvest' dining room is a classy-yet-comfortable venue to show off the wines and the essence of Clos Pegase. The pair of Baroque, serpentine columns—notice the grapevine theme—are from a French church of the 19th century, and are meant as a celebration of the symbol of the blood of Christ. The heels of your shoes click with a castle-like resonance on the terra cotta floor tiles.

At the entrance to the dining room is a fine bronze replica of the Renaissance Bacchus of

35

Michael Scranton, Wrecking Ball, 1989.

*Left: The longest of the cave
tunnels makes a dramatic
dinner for 250 people.*

*Right: The Harvest Dining
Room.*

Sansovino (1460-1529), the original in Venice. Above the fireplace is a large abstract painting by the Washington artist Sam Gilliam. On the opposite wall are murals, reproduced from a 15th century Book of Hours, depicting harvest scenes. The myriad-piece glass chandelier—meant to depict the rain drops that nourish the vines?—looks like it would take forever to properly dust and clean. They were put together by Mitsuko from glass links the Shrems obtained in Murano and which once graced their Parisian home, built by Napoleon for one of his Marshals. "You may notice that naughty Mitsuko broke Michael Graves' obsession with symmetry" whispers Jan in an artful stage aside. "Mitsuko didn't get along with our architect, who liked things orderly. The Greeks like symmetry, but the Japanese artistic sensibility rejects symmetry as boring and uninteresting. Beauty comes from tension. It jostles the mind, it makes you think. That, after all, is what all great art is about, yes?"

THE CAVES

There is something enchanting about a cave, any cave, but especially a wine cave, that reaches far beyond the mere utilitarian. The constancy of cool temperature and high humidity that allows barreled wines to age and mellow with significantly less evaporative loss than in warmer, drier air, and the tremendous energy savings that ensue from bypassing air conditioning: the wine cave offers a bewitching mix of the romantic,

The Cave Theatre, the ideal place to see Jan Shrem present "Bacchus the Rascal: A Bacchanalian History of Wine Seen Through 4,000 Years of Art."

Left: Antique wine bottles displayed in one of many sculpture niches in the cave system.

Right: The aging tunnels.

the magical, the mysterious, the practical. It is suggested that the humidity saves as much as a case of wine per barrel per year! Each barrel in the caves loses the equivalent of one case per year – in a dry environment, on the contrary, *two* cases would be lost!

Naturally, owner Jan Shrem had caves in mind when the winery was only an image in his fertile imagination. He was thrilled when his two-year search came up with this rugged knoll of volcanic *tufa* rock rising 150 feet above the valley floor. "Caves have been used artfully for aging wine for hundreds of years" he explains. "Indeed, there is copious evidence of extensive tunneling by the Etruscans beginning around 800 B.C. The Romans followed and surpassed the Etruscans with tunnels stretching for forty underground miles!" Remember, these were feats—the most remarkable underground outlets of Albano, Nemi, and Frecino Lakes—accomplished solely with pick and shovel.

"In Champagne, the Romans dug huge stone quarries that are still in use today for aging French sparkling wines. Likewise in the Loire Valley, stone quarries dug in the Middle Ages by French nobility

erecting their chateaux are now used for aging Loire wines."

When wine country's foremost cave digger Alf Bertleson put his oversized British mining machine—originally employed to root out coal mines—to work, the 22,000 square feet of new cave network instantly provided a constantly cool and comfortably humid home for the aging liquid art of Clos Pegase. The boring tool is a behemoth, with a rotating boom and a Medusa-like head that features 22 'arms' that bore into a hillside with a chilling efficiency.

When completed, the artistically high-ceilinged 2500-barrel space nearly equaled the 23,000 square feet of the wine facility. While special lighting serves to show off the inherent romance of the caves, the feature also enhances the caves' secondary purpose: as a site for winery events—like the famous 'Grapes of Laugh' comedy competitions the winery used to host, and Jan's extraordinary slide show depicting four millennia of wine in art, as only the impresario himself can present it—and as a further showplace for Jan's extensive art collection; Clos Pegase was, in fact,

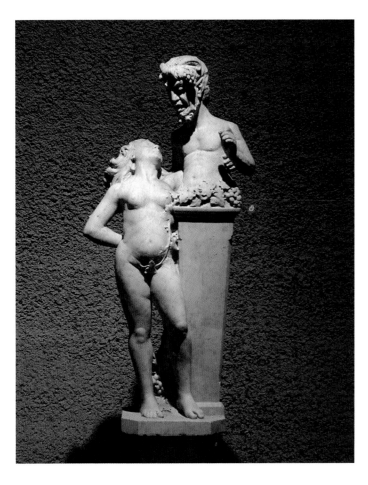

the first Napa Valley wine cave to also serve as art gallery. "Anthony Quinn celebrated his eightieth birthday in our cave theater by showing off his 2-year old daughter, and Gordon Getty rented this space to sing his opera *Plumpjack*. We have here cultural events, social events, corporate events…" says Jan.

As you walk through the cool, moss-less caverns—a hint of oak in your nostrils, near perfect acoustics echoing your footfall—you'll see niches populated by a Bacchus here, a collection of old bottles there, and other wine-related artistic treasures rendered in stone, *terra cotta* and marble. At the end of the main tunnel is an 18th century

marble from a northern French chateau that boasts a raw-yet-humorous realism: A young girl, hiding Bacchus' wine goblet behind her, teases a distraught Bacchus, denying him love…and wine to boot! The vaulted underground stage-and-theater—the surrounding niches display 18th and 19th century glassware, bottles and carafes of all sizes and shapes—can easily accommodate a dining audience of 120 guests, and more than 200 theatre-style.

Left: Bacchus Denied, 18th century French marble sculpture deep inside the cave tunnels. 150 feet directly above, through solid rock, is the Shrems' residence.

Right: A string quartet serenades diners in the caves.

17th Century Renaissance fountain, featuring four representations of Bacchus as an infant holding a dolphin, four Nymphs holding amphorae, and four Muses, each holding a different musical instrument.

THE VINEYARDS: THE FOUNTAINHEAD OF QUALITY

"The most important signs in any vineyard are the footprints of the winemaker."
–Andre Tchelistcheff

Think of it as a Greek chorus, chanting off to the side: "It all starts in the vineyard. If you haven't done it in the vineyard, you can't do it in the winery. Quality comes from the vine. Quality comes from the vine. Quality comes from the vine." There you have it, in the proverbial nutshell.

In the early renaissance of wine in California—the late sixties, all of the seventies—the production of wine had been essentially two different, indeed separate industries: the grape growers on the one hand (the sheepherders, if you will) and the winemakers (the cattlemen) on the other. The former farmed for quantity, in large part, while the latter aimed at quality.

The idea of the 'winegrower', in its best sense, is that the grower and the winemaker are, if not the same person, at least on the same side of the quality fence. Efforts like the 'bottle-price formula' for grape pricing were undertaken to compensate the growers for seeing that their 'product' was not grapes, but wine. When that happened—when yields were lowered, when leaves were stripped, when water was rationed—overall wine quality soared. And California became a 'player' at the highest level in the world's wine market.

Of the 450 acres owned by Jan and Mitsuko Shrem, nearly 300 are planted to the vine. Astutely, they have chosen four distinctively different sites, aiming to place each grape variety in exactly the right location. When the wine industry began its comeback in the 1960s, it was not uncommon to see varieties planted in the same vineyard… where ripening periods were different by fully *two months*! Chardonnay and Pinot Noir, for example, require a markedly cooler location than most varieties, preferably one closer to a large body of water which moderates temperature swings and allows for an uncommonly *even* ripening season. Cabernet Sauvignon is always the last one to the party, the last to mature its fruit, often making its grand appearance at the crush pad well into October.

A circumstance that only adds to the winemaker's good fortune—these are very good vineyards, after all—is the fact that up to a third of the fruit is sold to other luxury wine producers. What that means for winemaker Shaun Richardson is that he gets to cherry-pick his fruit, taking only

Spring shoot growth at Applebone Vineyard, surrounding the winery.

43

Robert Morris (b.1931) Three L Beams, 1965-1967, which took pride of place at the Guggenheim Museum in New York during a retrospective of the artist's works.

the best berries, making the best of an already delectable situation.

ESTATE BOTTLED: GROUND TO GLASS

While appellations—*where* the grapes are grown—are important, they are not the 'quality assurance' that most people want on a label.

The most important words on any wine label from a *quality* viewpoint are always those which name the producer. When someone has proven their reliability, over the years, their name is pretty much all you need to know about what's in the bottle.

There are, to be fair, two other label words that usually indicate a higher level of quality: 'Estate Bottled'. What that means is that the proprietor controls the fruit, from ground to glass. The only way to assure that what goes into the bottle is *exactly* the way you want it is to grow the grapes yourself. It's tough to ask an independent grower to strip leaves and thin fruit; it's a little easier to do—it remains hard to throw away perfectly good fruit—when the vines are yours and you know that the resulting wine quality 'bump up' will reflect well on your reputation.

"It is the cornerstone of our winemaking," says Shaun Richardson passionately. "Every wine we make is 'Estate Bottled.' We grow the grapes in our vineyards. We ferment the juice, we cellar the wine, we bottle the wine, and we put the Clos Pegase label on those bottles." The pride shows through, as it is meant to.

In line with that, Richardson recounts a tale told of the noted Christian Mouiex, proprietor of Pomerol's justly famed Chateau Petrus. "In the early 1970s Mouiex was walking one of his vineyards at the time of *veraison* (color change, berries turning from green to near-black). He understood that there was too much fruit on the vines for that season. Knowing that eventual fruit maturity might be threatened, he began cutting a few clusters off of each vine. Such a technique was unheard of at that time. He was dropping *money* on the ground or, more outrageously, as the local pastor pointed out to the congregation the following Sunday, he was destroying God's handiwork!"

Richardson adds, "Remember, a grape vine is physiologically quite simple: if it is dark all the time, it thinks it is in the forest and that it must produce more shoots and leaves to reach

Canadian geese at the Dunaweal Vineyard.

the sunlight. If the days are sunny, it thinks that producing all those shoots has worked well to get it to the top of the trees, and thus it should spend more energy on reproduction and setting fruit, so the birds will come and eat the grapes and spread the seeds in individual 'fertilizer packets'."

Richardson notes that one measure of the vine's behavior is the ratio of leaf-area-to-fruit weight; that is, comparing the amount of sunlight the plant converts to carbohydrates to the actual crop for a given season. The point of all this is that, when you control your own vineyards, you can take the 'risk' of dropping potential fruit on the ground when the reward of that lower crop is an optimized leaf area to fruit weight ratio, and dramatically improved flavor maturity, and thus fruit quality.

"Here in California, we have nutrition and sunlight in great abundance," continues Richardson, "which means that grape vines tend to produce too much fruit...because that is their genetic programming. Our job is to govern that growth, restrict it when necessary, to insure that the vine doesn't go crazy producing oversized berries and too much sugar. Thinning is a key aspect in quality winegrowing. Not only can we adjust the crop, but by removing the clusters that are unevenly colored, or have not completed veraison, we can achieve a more uniform ripening for the grapes that remain. Depending on the season, we might thin as little as five percent of the potential crop, or *as much as forty percent*." It is impossible to fairly ask that of an

46

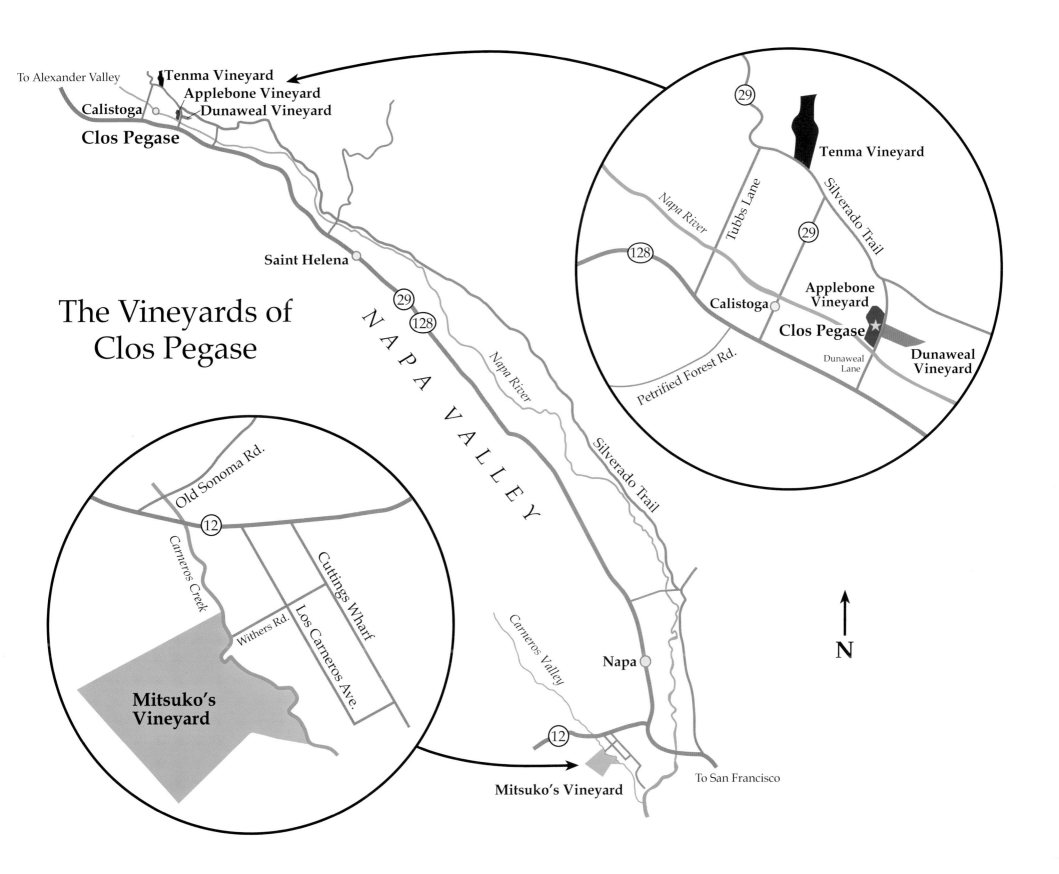

The Vineyards of Clos Pegase

To Alexander Valley

Tenma Vineyard
Applebone Vineyard
Dunaweal Vineyard

Calistoga

Clos Pegase

Saint Helena

29
128

NAPA VALLEY

Napa River

Silverado Trail

Carneros Valley

Napa

12

Mitsuko's Vineyard

To San Francisco

N

Inset (top right):

29

Tenma Vineyard

Napa River

Tubbs Lane

Silverado Trail

128

29

Calistoga

Applebone Vineyard

Clos Pegase

Petrified Forest Rd.

Dunaweal Lane

Dunaweal Vineyard

Inset (bottom left):

Old Sonoma Rd.

12

Carneros Creek

Withers Rd.

Cuttings Wharf

Los Carneros Ave.

Mitsuko's Vineyard

Varieties:
CF (Cab Franc) 6.75ac.
CS (Cab Sauv) 3.99ac.
PS (Petite Sirah) 1.80ac.
PV (Petit Verdot) 4.95ac.
SYR (Syrah) 1.04ac.
ZIN (Zinfandel) 3.59ac.

DUNAWEAL LN

APPLEBONE
VINEYARD

DUNAWEAL
VINEYARD

CS
0.57

CS
0.57

CS
2.85

PV
3.06

CF
3.06

PS
1.80

CF
3.69

PV
1.89

ZIN
1.70

ZIN
1.89

SYR
1.04

NDVI Values
Highest Vigor

Lowest Vigor
Fallow Land / Avenues

400   200   0   400
Feet

independent grower; it is absolutely imperative as a winegrower! That's why the term 'Estate Bottled' carries such weight in the marketplace of great wines.

"The notion of the 'Estate' is common among the First Growths of France," he notes, "and starting to catch on here. We see it with such estates as Screaming Eagle and Dominus (a Mouiex property), as well as many great 'Estate Bottled' wines from wineries which also purchase fruit, like our neighbor Chateau Montelena. What 'Estate Bottled' says to the consumer is that the winery takes as much care in the evolution of the raw material—the grapes—as it does in the actual making of the wine."

THE VINEYARDS

DUNAWEAL VINEYARD(formerly 'Home Ranch' Vineyard)

"We bought this 26-acre vineyard—directly across the street from the winery—along with the winery site in 1983," says Shrem. "We originally planted Sauvignon Blanc on the deep Bale clay-

loam, but it didn't do all that well." Grape vines don't like 'wet feet,' and this site was prone to holding water. Extensive soil and drainage work had to be done before the site was replanted to Petit Verdot and Cabernet Franc in 1992 and expanded in 1998.

Seven acres of Cabernet Franc and five acres of Petit Verdot cover most of the land, with a little over three acres of Zinfandel, nearly two of Petite Sirah, and one acre of Syrah.

APPLEBONE VINEYARD

This is the vineyard immediately adjacent to the winery named after the Mark Di Suvero sculpture that graces the property. Originally planted to Merlot, *phylloxera* (the American root louse that decimated European vineyards in the late 1800's) became a problem here at the end of the last century. The rootstock the Merlot was grafted to, AXR1, turned out to be notorious for its susceptibility to *phylloxera*. Four acres of the 20-acre site were graded in 2000; new resistant rootstocks were planted the following year, and then budded to Cabernet Sauvignon in 2002.

Opposite: The Normalized Digital Vegetation Index (NDVI) shows the differing levels of planting density at Applebone (4' between rows and 4' between vines) and Dunaweal Vineyards (8' x 5'): the higher leaf area at Applebone registering as greater vigor.

Above: Mark Di Suvero (b. 1933) Applebone, 1986-1987.

Above: The exacting care of the grape harvest.

Opposite: Mitsuko's Vineyard, where the NDVI vividly shows the recently planted areas of vineyard, and within the older parcels, the more subtle vigor changes due to natural swales and soil changes.

"The soils here are identical to those of our Dunaweal Vineyard, across the street," says Richardson, "so they tend to produce overly vigorous vines, and we had to address this to suppress Cabernet's natural vigor. If the site allows it, vines can get carried away growing leaves, to the point of putting fruit maturity off almost entirely. So we planted at a very high density with vines four feet apart. This forces them to compete against each other for nutrition and water, and to focus more of their attention on maturing the grape berries and not just growing wonderfully green leaves in great profusion."

MITSUKO'S VINEYARD

Carnero is the Spanish word for 'ram', so it is hardly any surprise that this cool area of the

Napa Valley was originally sheep country. With its proximity to the cold San Francisco Bay, Beaulieu's vaunted winemaker Andre Tchelistcheff touted the region for its cold-climate varieties, and claimed that the best wine he ever made was the BV 1946 Carneros Pinot Noir. Since then, we have learned that other varieties—Chardonnay, Merlot, and even Cabernet Sauvignon if it's on well-drained soil—can also do better than well in this bay-cooled, thin-soiled appellation.

"Keep in mind, this was originally an extension of the San Francisco Bay," notes Richardson "and the region is largely covered with a three-foot layer of heavy clay soils. The dairy farmer that we bought the property from went out of his way to point out his favorite small piece of the farm, a low hill that when plowed, turned up large

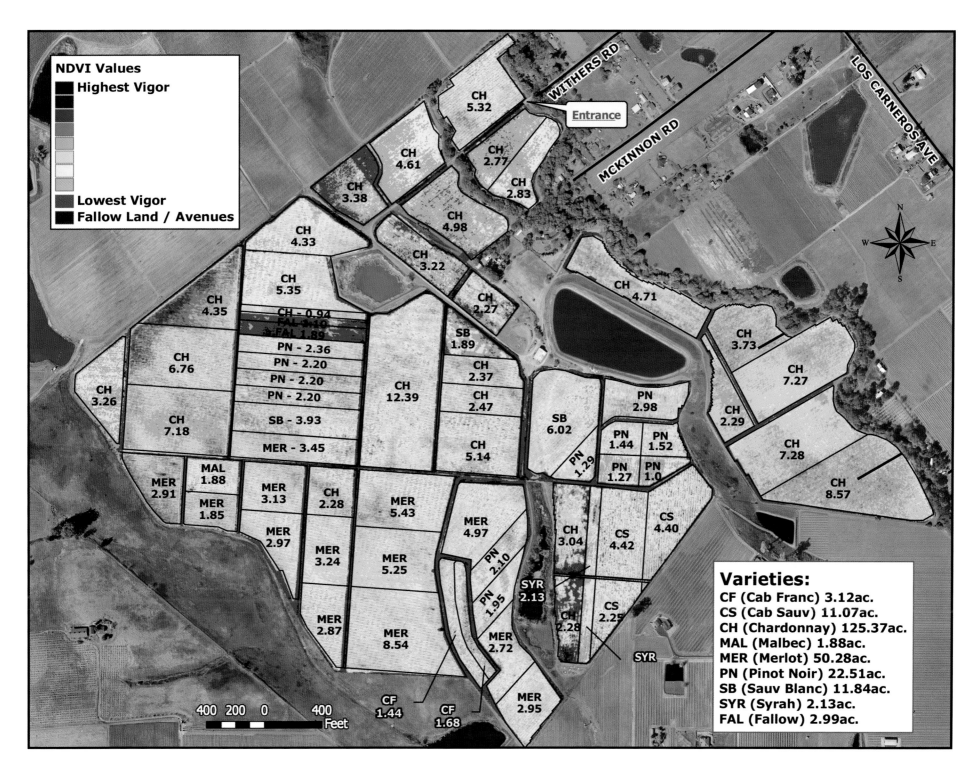

NDVI Values
Highest Vigor

Lowest Vigor
Fallow Land / Avenues

WITHERS RD
MCKINNON RD
LOS CARNEROS AVE

Entrance

CH 5.32
CH 4.61
CH 2.77
CH 2.83
CH 3.38
CH 4.98
CH 4.33
CH 3.22
CH 5.35
CH 2.27
CH 4.35
CH – 0.94
FAL 1.10
FAL 1.89
PN – 2.36
PN – 2.20
PN – 2.20
PN – 2.20
SB – 3.93
MER – 3.45
CH 6.76
CH 3.26
CH 7.18
CH 12.39
SB 1.89
CH 2.37
CH 2.47
CH 5.14
CH 4.71
CH 3.73
CH 7.27
CH 2.29
CH 7.28
CH 8.57
SB 6.02
PN 2.98
PN 1.44
PN 1.52
PN 1.29
PN 1.27
PN 1.0
MAL 1.88
MER 2.91
MER 1.85
MER 3.13
CH 2.28
MER 5.43
MER 4.97
CH 3.04
CS 4.42
CS 4.40
MER 2.97
MER 3.24
MER 5.25
PN 2.10
SYR 2.13
CH 2.28
CS 2.25
MER 2.87
MER 8.54
PN 1.95
MER 2.72
SYR
CF 1.44
CF 1.68
MER 2.95

400 200 0 400 Feet

Varieties:
CF (Cab Franc) 3.12ac.
CS (Cab Sauv) 11.07ac.
CH (Chardonnay) 125.37ac.
MAL (Malbec) 1.88ac.
MER (Merlot) 50.28ac.
PN (Pinot Noir) 22.51ac.
SB (Sauv Blanc) 11.84ac.
SYR (Syrah) 2.13ac.
FAL (Fallow) 2.99ac.

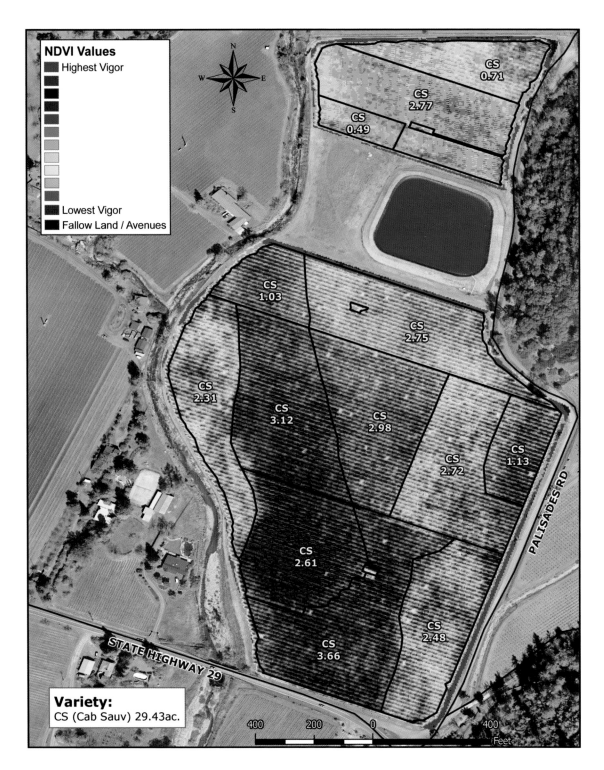

broken white cobbles, looking for all the world like disturbed tombs. Following his lead, we took to calling that piece Graveyard Hill. It is a special piece – only 11 acres – that we have planted to Cabernet Sauvignon…and we can actually ripen that variety there, despite the cool Carneros climate! As opposed to the heavy Carneros clay, there is a ten-foot deep layer of cobbled soil; a profile more commonly found in Howell Mountain: the excellent drainage allows the soil to warm up earlier in the spring, giving bud break and flowering a head start, which extends the growing season just long enough for this late-ripening variety."

Most of Mitsuko's Vineyard is planted to Chardonnay (123 acres), with smaller allotments of Merlot (51 acres), Pinot Noir (23 acres), the

Cabernet Sauvignon on Graveyard Hill (11 acres), Sauvignon Blanc (12 acres), Cabernet Franc (three acres) and Syrah (two acres). The vineyard was acquired as bare pastureland in 1989 and planting was begun in 1991.

TENMA VINEYARD (formerly 'Palisades' Vineyard)

This is the jewel in the crown, according to all at the winery. "This austere vineyard is an alluvial fan that spills out of the Palisades range in the north-easternmost corner of the Napa Valley," says Richardson, calling a vivid picture of the site to mind. "The Calistoga AVA is the warmest area of the Napa Valley in the summer, but it's also the coolest in the winter and gets half again as much rain—thirty-six inches—as the southern part of the valley. It's something of a balancing act. The

Tenma site is also a unique part of Calistoga that receives more fog in summer due to the influence of the Russian River gap, and is thus slightly cooler than Applebone and Dunaweal vineyards further south."

Simply enough, the soils are poor and dry, and deeply-drained, which means that crop levels are inordinately low. That leads inevitably to marvelously concentrated fruit expression. You don't get as much fruit as you'd like, but what is harvested is exquisite, and the stony terrain produces some of the finest Cabernet Sauvignon in the entire valley, with superb aromatics and wonderfully plummy, ripe fruit flavors. The parcel covers 42 acres, most, 29 acres, are planted to what it's best suited to; that is to say all are given over to Cabernet Sauvignon. You don't mess with

Fall at Applebone Vineyard.

Opposite: Tenma Vineyard (formerly Palisades). With constant vine and row spacing, this NDVI shows the dramatic soil variations in the area south of the reservoir, from low vigor vines on rocky soil, to high vigor vines on clay-loam.

Farming meets modernism:
John Deere meets Jean
Dubuffet.

perfection.

"I first bought the property in 1987," says Shrem, "originally planted to some Cabernet and smaller amounts of Merlot, Cabernet Franc and Petite Sirah. We quickly realized the potential of the site and expanded the Cabernet Sauvignon and removed the other, less successful varieties." Richardson goes on to explain the site further. "We always struggled with lack of water, so recently we took out three acres of vines for a reservoir, primarily to allow us to maintain the vine water-status later into the season and achieve greater levels of ripeness. Dry-farmed, we were giving up a little too much of the flavor potential of the fruit; dry farming is very romantic in theory, but we found that if we left fruit hanging to achieve maximum ripeness, it started to shrivel before that point. With a judicious use of water from

the reservoir, maximum ripeness is possible, and we may even get more fruit from this hard stony ground. Any additional fruit we get is, of course, a bonus, but the goal is always to grow better fruit. And it is *very good fruit!*" With such a dramatic change in the quality of the fruit due to the reservoir, a name change was in order: Tenma is Japanese for Pegasus.

TOM PRENTICE: CONSULTING VITICULTURIST

Famed viticultural consultant Tom Prentice—his company, Crop Care, was founded in 1970—was brought on board in 2006 to determine what would be necessary in time to nudge fruit quality at Tenma to the highest possible level. The wine industry is particularly good at this. One winery owner noted that his job was to do things that the president of the company "a hundred years from

54

now would thank me for having done."

"Water was the big limiting factor, so putting in a reservoir was a great move by Jan and Shaun," says Prentice, who grew up in a grape farming family in Madera and Fresno, but took his degree from UC Berkeley in History. "With moisture stress late in the growing season, it's hard to get the fruit to its fullest maturity."

Another key aspect of Prentice's approach is the attention to detail to the current plantings, which has made a very significant contribution to the quality gains seen most recently. The Tenma vines can now almost be called 'manicured', rather than farmed.

Prentice has also directed a change in vine orientation (for new planting), shifting rows from northwest-southeast to northeast-southwest. He says: "This gives the vines a little more morning sunlight and a bit less afternoon sunlight, which

is better for the vines. We will also change the trellising to a more vertical system, which spreads out the light beneficially, and go to a much closer vine spacing (seven feet by four feet), which will allow us to lower the crop level to four or five pounds per vine, but keep the overall crop level per acre at a healthy point. The fact that Jan is looking at this as a twelve year project is a very European way of thinking, being willing to pay now for a quality improvement that won't be fully realized until further down the road. The collaboration here—with Shaun, who is a pleasure to work with, with Paul Hobbs, with whom I have worked easily with before on other projects, and with Pegase's former winemaker Bill Pease who's now at Madrigal Vineyard Management (the people who actually do the work)—has been very productive. These are really professional people, and the positive results here show it."

The south-facing entrance portico seen over the close-planted vines of Applebone Vineyard.

55

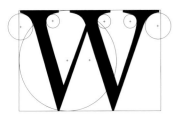

THE WINES OF CLOS PEGASE

"Foolish eyes, thy streams give over wine, not water, binds the lover; at the table then be shining, gay coquette, and all designing." – *English poet Martha Sansom (1690-1736)*

Wine is perhaps the most basic, most perfect gift that Nature offers to mankind. Its very existence is nothing less than providential accident. Some ancient Persian, in overfilling his fired-clay *olla* with grapes, allowed those berries at the bottom to be broken. When the yeast on the skins came into contact with the sugar-rich juice, fermentation began. Sugars were broken down into ethanol and carbon dioxide. Nonetheless, the ensuing liquid tasted good. It made food taste better. It improved conversation. Its alcohol not only preserved the liquid, it gave rise to pleasing feelings of happiness and contentment. To say the least, it was a discovery of some note!

TO BE MOST HAPPY, YOU START WITH FOOD

"You start with food," stresses Shrem. He is fairly adamant about this. "We knew when we started that we could make big, bold wines. What we didn't know was if we could build wines that had the substance we wanted, but also the structure—yes, the architectural structure—to stand appropriately alongside artfully prepared cuisine. If we couldn't do that, well, it might not have been worth the effort to even begin the project."

Given that desire, Jan did the smartest thing he could have done. Even before winery construction was underway, he hired consulting winemaker Andre Tchelistcheff, the Russian who made his reputation at Beaulieu Vineyard over a period of nearly four decades and served as guru to numerous wineries (most notably Jordan and Chateau Ste. Michelle). "Andre has fantastic powers," noted Warren Winiarski, founder of Stag's Leap Wine Cellars, for whom Andre also consulted. "He can be imperious, abrupt, impatient with sloppy procedures, but he is also poetic, visionary, romantic. He is possessed by two geniuses: dry-eyed, rigorous exactitude, and generous leaps of imagination—non-rigid, non-uniform and innovative."

That's the precise way of explaining the breadth of Tchelistcheff's experience—in France and in California—and how rooted to the earth

The Pegasus graces the label of all wines other than the Hommage series. Each of the Hommage labels comes from art in the Clos Pegase collection.

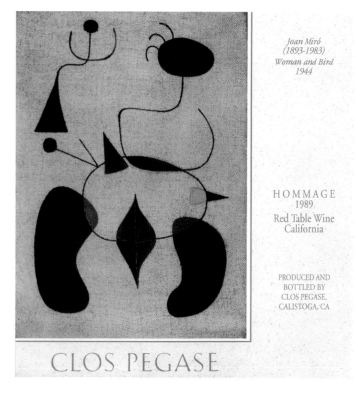

The art collection of Clos Pegase consists of 300 paintings. With two pieces selected each year for the Hommage program, the Shrems have thoughtfully planned for Clos Pegase to exist for the next 150 years!

Left: Salvador Dali (1904-1989) Surrealist Composition, 1928.

Right: Joan Miró (1893-1983) Woman and Bird, 1944.

that experience and knowledge always was. Andre said over and over that "the most tell-tale mark in any vineyard was the footprint of the winemaker." If you don't know the vineyard, you cannot know its wines. Basic? Yep. Essential? Absolutely.

Pegase's first winemaker, Bill Pease, always emphasized that he was going for character over size. "Europe has been growing grapes for wine for thousands of years, and we have little more than a hundred and fifty years here. Our soils are far more fertile than those in Europe, so we have to work a little harder to make wines with delicacy rather than brute force. Size is easy; complexity is hard."

In a casual conversation, I once asked Jan if he had any intention of increasing production, given the success the wines have achieved. He laughed:

"We are not interested in working any harder than we already are!"

THE WHITE WINES OF CLOS PEGASE

SAUVIGNON BLANC

Sauvignon Blanc is one of the most food-friendly white varietals grown on the third rock from the sun. Where there is bracing natural fruit acidity to rein in the fruit, this wine can handle anything from the subtlety of a buttered filet of sole to the briskness of a barbecued pork chop. Rhetorical question: Name another white varietal that can handle that range?

"The particular climate-soil mix of our Carneros vineyard—a coolish, bay-influenced climate, the Haire clay-loam soils—is what makes

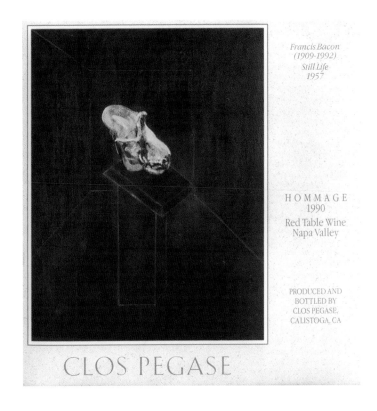

Sauvignon Blanc work for us," says Richardson. "Grape acidity is an element in this wine, but more importantly, we factor the way the grapes taste into our picking decisions. We're looking for rich fruit expression in the finished wine, but when making the harvest decision, there's no particular flavor marker that appears, rather, there is only the slow decrease of the methoxy-pyrazines, the bell pepper notes. If you don't have both, liveliness on the palate, and flavor—the wine is going to be dull and uninteresting. We pick our fruit fairly ripe, but it still has the necessary vibrancy."

As it is, the Mitsuko's Vineyard Sauvignon Blanc fairly bristles with crisp lime, grapefruit and pineapple fruitiness, with hints of other tropical flavors: kiwi, gooseberry and honeydew melon. There are also those wonderfully earthy fig

and hay scents that only add to the richness and complexity of the wine and add to its ability to master so many cuisines. The whole Asian "fusion" scene was made for this wine, which is doing so well for Clos Pegase that production is inching upwards from 2,000 cases per year to double that.

The Sauvignon Musque clone used at Clos Pegase is known for its tangy spiciness and its aromatics—thus the Muscat relation in name. The wine does not undergo malolactic fermentation so as to retain its vital freshness, and is aged only five months in the cellar. One-third resides in stainless steel and the remainder in large, 130 gallon French oak puncheons. Billon is the cooper, from Burgundy, and the small percentage of new oak integrates merely as an accent. In smaller barrels, the oak would intrude, dimming the wine's fresh

Left: Francis Bacon (1909-1992) Still Life, 1957.

Right: Max Ernst (1891-1976) Surrealist Composition, 1953.

Sam Francis
(1923-1994)
Composition
1957

HOMMAGE
1992
Artist Series Reserve
Cabernet Sauvignon
Napa Valley

PRODUCED AND
BOTTLED BY
CLOS PEGASE,
CALISTOGA, CA
ALC. 12.5% BY VOL.

CLOS PEGASE

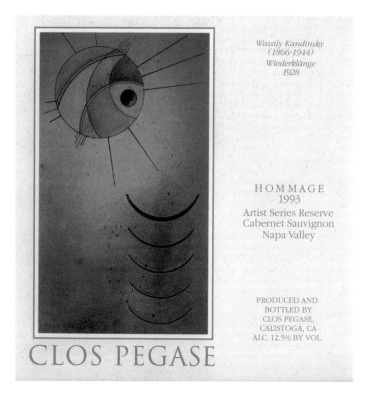

Wassily Kandinsky
(1866-1944)
Wiederklänge
1928

HOMMAGE
1993
Artist Series Reserve
Cabernet Sauvignon
Napa Valley

PRODUCED AND
BOTTLED BY
CLOS PEGASE,
CALISTOGA, CA
ALC. 12.5% BY VOL.

CLOS PEGASE

Left: Sam Francis (1923-1994) Composition, 1957.

Right: Wassily Kandinsky (1866-1944) Wiederklänge, 1928.

zestiness.

Since the 2002 vintage, the wine has been finished with a screw cap, "It's more user-friendly," says Richardson, "and you don't have nearly the spoilage problems. When we started counting rejection problems from all the bottles opened in our own tasting room, nearly five percent of our cork-finished wines were rejected; a few for the obvious musty cork-taint aroma, and many for random oxidation, caused no doubt by cork's natural variability. That violates our business sensibility: why would you want to send out a product that is potentially faulty in any way?"

CHARDONNAY

Once something of a miscreant 'problem child' in California—because winemakers thought

they could do *anything* with the grape, often overloading the varietal with excessive alcohol and oak—Chardonnay is enjoying a modest rebirth at wineries where fruit and balance are honored and promoted.

You see, this Burgundian beauty is capable of offering so much more when its inherent fruit is allowed to show through. "As with all the varieties, when we pick the grapes, we're looking at the overall health of the vine, the sugar and acid levels, the physical softness of the fruit, and the complexity of the flavors. Oak is a framework for the wine, but not its reason for existing," says Richardson. "It is there *not* to overwhelm the wine, but to give it extra dimension. We want our Chardonnay to be enjoyable and refreshing; we want people to drink it with dinner. All of

60

Wilfredo Lam
(1902-1982)
The Oracle
and the Green Bird
1947

HOMMAGE
1994
Artist Series Reserve
Cabernet Sauvignon
Napa Valley

GROWN, PRODUCED
& BOTTLED BY
CLOS PEGASE,
CALISTOGA, CA
ALC. 13.5% BY VOL.

CLOS PEGASE

Yves Tanguy
(1900-1955)
Surrealist Composition
1940

HOMMAGE
1995
Artist Series Reserve
Cabernet Sauvignon
Napa Valley

GROWN, PRODUCED
& BOTTLED BY
CLOS PEGASE,
CALISTOGA, CA
ALC. 13.5% BY VOL.

CLOS PEGASE

the Chardonnay always goes through malolactic fermentation, converting the malic acid to lactic acid: we downplay the influence of this by using a selection of malolactic bacteria that does not produce diacetyl, the buttered popcorn aroma which is a natural by-product of the process. It helps to focus the wine on the fruit, yet also allows it to benefit from the creamy texture, another by-product, increasing the complexity of the wine."

That approach leads to a wine that shows off juicy, sappy Fuji apple and pear fruitiness, with cream and vanillin and hazelnut impressions from the oak, and a texture that is creamy and rich. "I always like the peach and nectarine notes that are there with the apple and pear" adds Richardson. "The acid-to-alcohol balance is a key factor, and the texture only gets better after three or four years."

Chicken in a cream sauce is an obvious choice to pair with this wine, but a nice veal shank would also be shown off to its best lights. Your favorite oriental dishes would also match well with the thick texture of the Mitsuko's Vineyard Chardonnay.

THE RED WINES OF CLOS PEGASE

PINOT NOIR

Pinot Noir is universally renowned as the 'Golden Fleece' of wine: impossible to attain, irresistible to attempt. It is something of the 'ideal,' created in the mind to a degree of perfection that is unattainable in the real world. Yet we try, because the ideal is so alluring. All you have to say is "liquid sensuality," and every nerve in your body is immediately attuned to what *might* be possible.

*Left: Wilfredo Lam
(1902-1982) The Oracle and
the Green Bird, 1947.*

*Right: Yves Tanguy
(1900-1955) Surrealist
Composition, 1940.*

61

Francis Picabia
(1879-1953)
*The Man with the
Red Gloves
1923-25*

HOMMAGE
1996
Artist Series
RESERVE
Napa Valley
Red Wine

Grown, produced and
bottled by
CLOS PEGASE
Calistoga, CA
Alc. 13.5% by volume

CLOS PEGASE

Oscar Dominguez
(1906 - 1957)
*Les Papillons
(1943)*

HOMMAGE
1997
Artist Series
RESERVE
Cabernet Sauvignon
Napa Valley

Estate Bottled
CLOS PEGASE
Calistoga, CA
Alc. 14.3% by Volume

CLOS PEGASE

*Left: Francis Picabia
(1879-1953) The Man with the
Red Gloves, 1923-25.*

*Right: Oscar Dominguez
(1906-1957) Les Papillons,
1943.*

You see, Pinot Noir is all about wines whose sensual textural attributes are nearly lascivious, even libidinous in nature. Part of the Pinot's mystique is that it is—at one and the same time—the most precious of winedom's prizes and the most pixilating of its puzzles. So, while great Pinot Noirs stand apart from all other red table wines in their sweeping grandeur, so too is the grape variety quarrelsome as the devil: as a vine, as a maturing grape, as fermenting must and as aging wine.

Getting the right grape plant is a pain in the backside, as there are thousands of clones to choose from, and then you have to put the right clone in that certain patch of ground that best suits its demands. As with Chardonnay, Pinot Noir is susceptible to all sorts of viral diseases; and as

with Chardonnay, this can be one of the keys to the wine's greatness, or its downfall. It turns out that the wily Pinot's complexity is well earned: A team of French and Italian researchers recently mapped the variety's genome and its DNA has some 30,000 genes and 500 million chemical building blocks. In contrast, the human genome only contains 20-25,000 genes!

"The overriding key with Pinot Noir," acknowledges Richardson, "is planting it in the right place – it is the variety most critically allied to *terroir.*" Taste the wines and you will see. The Clos Pegase Pinot Noirs are silken-textured lovelies that meld red and black cherry fruit with a filet mignon meatiness that is seductive to the extreme. Add to that the spiciness of cardamom and an almost crisp bacon-like oak framework.

Alfred Wols
(1913-1951)
Le Bateau Ivre

HOMMAGE
1997
Artist Series
RESERVE
CHARDONNAY
Carneros • Napa Valley
Mitsuko's Vineyard

GROWN, PRODUCED
& BOTTLED BY
CLOS PEGASE
CALISTOGA, CA
ALC. 14.0% BY VOLUME

CLOS PEGASE

Otto Freundlich
(1878-1943)
Ghetto
1936

HOMMAGE
1998
Artist Series
RESERVE
Chardonnay
Carneros • Napa Valley
Mitsuko's Vineyard

Estate Bottled
CLOS PEGASE
Calistoga, CA
Alc. 14.2% by Volume

CLOS PEGASE

MERLOT

In France, we know Merlot for the "pretty" velvet softness of St. Emilion and the self-contained power of Pomerol. In California, we first knew the variety as the flesh to Cabernet's bones in blends of the two, perfected over centuries in several regions of old Gaul.

Richardson likes the Carneros for Merlot. "It was once thought to be too cold a climate for Merlot, but when you plant the variety on the right soil, you get a wine of elegance that really shows off the region. Andre Tchelistcheff recommended we plant the variety at Mitsuko's Vineyard and I think it was one of his best suggestions."

Typically, the Clos Pegase Merlot shows off a mélange of red and black fruit character, from red cherry and cranberry, to black currant and cassis.

A little Cabernet Franc, for aromatics, and Petit Verdot, for color and intensity, are often added to the blend for additional layers of interest and complexity.

"We use natural yeast for Merlot, and in fact for all the red wines, which gives the wine greater complexity in flavor and a real sense of the 'place' the grapes come from," says Richardson. "Specifically, we give a third of the wine extended skin contact. For another third we do drain and return—called *delestage*—for greater extraction, and another third is pressed early to help retain the inherent vibrancy that Merlot is so known for."

CABERNET SAUVIGNON

The 'King' of Bordeaux, Cabernet Sauvignon has always been the best known varietal in this

Left: Alfred Wols (1913-1951) Le Bateau Ivre.

Right: Otto Freundlich (1878-1943) Ghetto, 1936.

country, from the wonderfully ageable Rutherford standards crafted by Andre Tchelistcheff and George Deuer from the 1950s onward for Beaulieu and Inglenook, respectively, to the elegantly constructed wines of Louis Martini in the same time period and the bold assessments of Robert Mondavi, starting in 1966. Later, Jordan and Rodney Strong would emerge on the Sonoma side of the Mayacamas range, and the race would be joined on all sides.

The Texans called it "Cabernet Son-of-a-Gun," and others kidded with "Life is a Cabernet," but the bottom line is that no matter where the variety is grown, when it is well-matched to terroir and well-made in the cellar it is a wine of clear and defined personality and well-noted distinction. There is nothing hesitant about the wine we call

"Cab."

Cabernet is important at Clos Pegase, and Richardson knows what he's doing with it. The Napa Valley Cabernet Sauvignon is imposing and assertive, with cassis and currant galore, with brightly announced dark chocolate and blackberry notes that serve to push the core fruit forward, as a well-chosen frame gives a great painting yet more currency and weight.

Cabernet Sauvignon winemaking is straightforward—get everything possible out of the grapes by harvesting fully ripe fruit, then extract with vigor during the fermentation and maceration on skins. *Elevage* of the wines in barrel improves on the harvest: after maximizing the extract and tannin, and wines are racked frequently to build greater structure and suppleness. Using 45% new

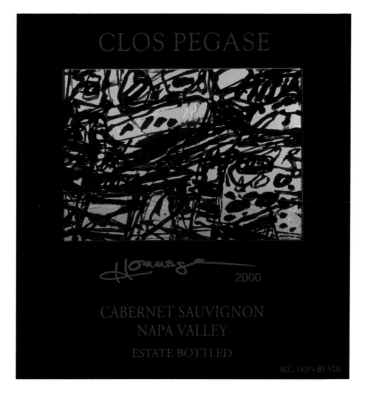

oak for the Napa Valley blend gives even greater complexity and mouthfeel.

JUST FOR FUN

Tasting room guests and Wine Club members also garner the benefit of Richardson's typically Aussie nature, which is playful and eclectic. Hence the small lots of wines like Cabernet Franc (more often used in Cabernet and Merlot blends) and Syrah, all estate-grown. The former shows off the vibrant aromatics typical of Cabernet Franc, with pepper and raspberry, red currant and violets. "That dusty tannin really gives a lift to the texture of the Franc," says Richardson, "and gives it vibrancy in the mouth, in the finish."

Of the Syrah, he likes the lively, bright strawberry, black pepper and blackberry fruit that

is quick in the nose and long-lasting in the mouth. This is your fireplace wine, with a nice plate of sharp Cheddar and good knife to keep guests well supplied with a slice or two along with the Syrah. This is the variety, of course, that is better known as Shiraz in Australia, where it is that country's vinous signature.

THE ARTIST SERIES: HOMMAGE

HOMMAGE CHARDONNAY

Hommage is exactly what the word sounds like, an honoring of the best lots of the best grapes from the best vineyards. There is one white *Hommage* each vintage, and there is one red *Hommage*. "It is taking what we are already proud of, and taking it to the max," says Shrem succinctly. "Each year

Left: Amédée Ozenfant (1886-1966) Nature Morte Puriste, 1925.

Right: Jean Dubuffet (1901-1985) Mire G53, 1983.

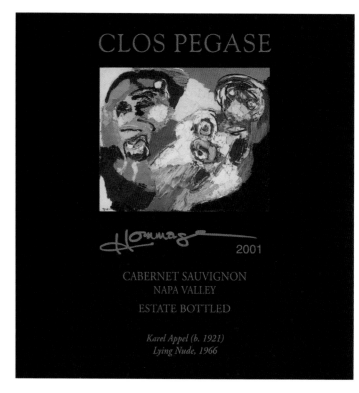

we choose a different painting from our collection to pay homage to the memory of the artist with the best wine we can offer to his memory. It is, of course, more than that."

The Chardonnay *Hommage* is from Mitsuko's Vineyard. "With our *Hommage* wines we are operating under the 'more is better' principle," acknowledges Richardson. "These are 'Show' wines, designed to impress, and designed to show off the quality of our vineyards. Mitsuko's Vineyard is a world-class vineyard, as is Tenma: the Hommage wines are targeted to express this. When we taste through what we have in the winery after harvest, we select the best, most concentrated barrels for the *Hommage* program. With the Chardonnay, the wine gets *twice* the time in oak: sixteen months as opposed to the eight

months of our regular Chardonnay. In addition, twice as much of the wine (two-thirds) is aged in new oak. That, obviously, makes for a richer, more pronounced texture, and additional oak character." Shrem adds: "Hommage is a double selection, first in the vineyard, and second from what we find best in the barrels, the cream of the cream. It is our signature offering," and with a chuckle, "A double selection at double the price, of course."

Indeed, the *Hommage* Chardonnay is chockablock with hazelnut and fresh French bread bakery smells and flavors, along with the thick, creamy richness of fruit expression that you would also expect, again with apple, pear, peach and nectarine in profusion. It is a gorgeous, voluptuous wine, truly amped-up, yes, but all of its elements retaining the on-pitch balance that is essential for

CLOS PEGASE

Hommage 2002

MITSUKO'S VINEYARD
CHARDONNAY
CARNEROS • NAPA VALLEY

ESTATE BOTTLED

Manolo Millares (1926-1972)
Cuadro III, 1961

CLOS PEGASE

Hommage 2002

CABERNET SAUVIGNON
NAPA VALLEY

ESTATE BOTTLED

Jean Dubuffet (1901-1985)
Site avec 4 personnages, 1981

such a wine to age out gracefully in bottle.

The Hommage Chardonnay typically comes from the Wente clone, and there's more to that throw-away comment than meets the eye. Cuttings from that old Livermore family's vines were first brought to the Napa Valley by Dartmouth grad Fred McCrea at Stony Hill in 1948. The way Fred always told the story was this: "When I got the cuttings from the Wentes, Ernest (the vineyardist) direly told me that the vines were *exceedingly* shy-bearing, while Herman (the family's winemaker) advised me that the wines were wonderfully concentrated in flavor. They were both right!"

HOMMAGE CABERNET SAUVIGNON

"The richness of the fruit balances out the hearty tannins and the 'healthy' alcohol," says Richardson about Clos Pegase's justly prized *Hommage Cabernet Sauvignon.* "We're looking to make the absolutely richest and most intense red wine. We're not looking for a consistent style, but simply to take the best fruit we're given from the season and extend it to be the best Cabernet possible for each different vintage."

When you taste the wine, you come face-to-face with more-than-ample portions of black currant, blackberry, cassis, tobacco and blackberry fruit—sometimes a little menthol, a little peppermint—enough graham oak to highlight the fruit without impinging upon it, and plenty of black pepper spiciness that tries to keep all of that fruit inside the frame. No small trick, that. Nearly impossible, in fact. Nearly.

Though occasionally the elegant cool-climate

Left: Manolo Millares (1926-1972) Cuadro III, 1961.

Right: Jean Dubuffet (1901-1985) Site avec 4 personnages, 1981.

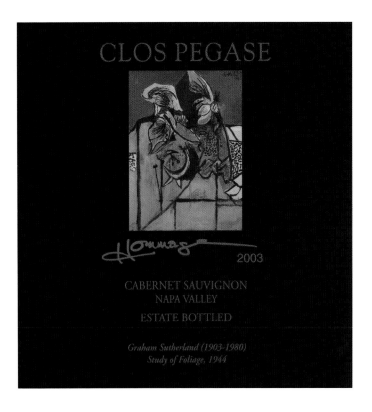

Left: Graham Sutherland (1903-1980) Study of Foliage, 1944.

Right: Roberto Matta (1911-2002) Les Amoureuses, 1947.

fruit from Carneros is employed to blend with the ripe, jammy fruit up-valley, Tenma Vineyard is at the very heart of the wine. "This vineyard washes down through Jericho Canyon and has virtual 'stripes' of visible rock and clay and boulders running through it," says Richardson, with a contagious passion for the site in his inflection. "There are fifteen different blocks, covering a wide array of different soil types and textures. You can actually see five different zones in one vine-row! In some areas, the difference in harvest time can be up to two or three weeks. It's a grower's nightmare, but a winemaker's dream!"

PAUL HOBBS: CONSULTING WINEMAKER

Hobbs was introduced to Clos Pegase in mid-2006 to help change the direction of and improve the quality of the Cabernet program, specifically with Tenma Vineyard, and is thrilled to be working with the fruit. "I had never seen the vineyard prior to working with Jan, though I had worked with nearby properties on other consulting projects," says the curly-haired, blue-eyed Hobbs. "There was the myth that Calistoga is a very warm vineyard location, but the afternoon breezes that filter down Highway 128 belie that notion. (Napa Valley actually extends northwest to the Pacific Ocean, by way of Alexander Valley and Anderson Valley, otherwise known as the Russian River gap.) It also helps that—with the new reservoir—we have water available on demand. That changes everything. It's like a marathon, and you run out of gas two miles from the finish line. When you've got water, and the growing season is a dry one, you

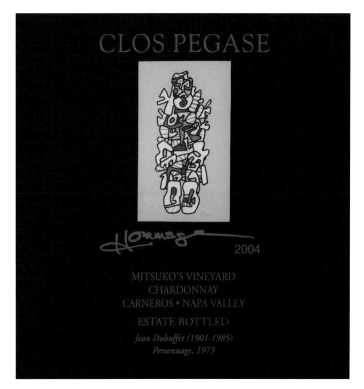

can keep the vines from conking out before we get to our finish line, harvest. You don't want to run out of water even a mile short of the finish line."

"Working with Shaun and Tom Prentice," he explains, "we've done a major overhaul on Tenma vineyard, and fine-tuned certain aspects of pruning and canopy management. There is still a lot of replanting yet to do. We're going to work with different clones to increase our blending opportunities. There's still a lot to be done, but we've already seen extraordinary results from what we've accomplished thus far."

"In the winery, we're focusing on better, individual berry selection—the sorting table is a big help—gentler handling of the fruit, more careful fruit maceration, and better tannin management. All of this leads to an increase in

subtlety and elegance in the finished product. All you have to do is try the wines. You can taste the differences!"

Paul Hobbs is an intelligent winemaker. Growing up on an apple farm in Niagara County, upstate New York, one of eleven children, Hobbs has created an impressive consulting empire. He studied pre-med at Notre Dame University before coming to the conclusion that grape farming was in his blood. So he came to California, studied at UC Davis, and apprenticed at Robert Mondavi and Simi, there working closely with renowned consultant Zelma Long. He has a dozen clients of his own in the U.S., a half dozen in Argentina, about the same in Chile, a couple in Hungary ("beautiful sweet wines") and even one in Armenia! In addition, he has his own

Left: Richard Lindner (1901-1978) Girl with Hoop, 1969.

Right: Jean Dubuffet (1901-1985) Personnage, 1973.

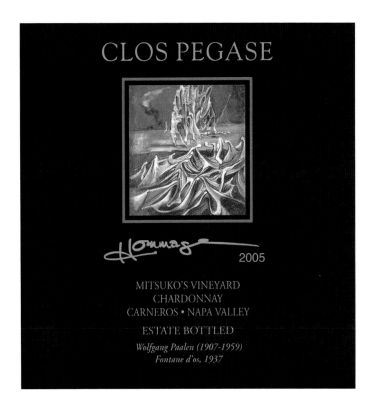

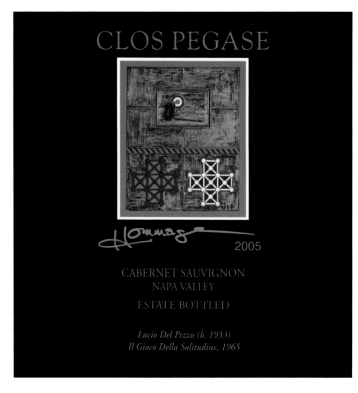

small eponymous winery in Sonoma County's Russian River Valley—mostly local Pinot Noir and Chardonnay, but a small amount of Napa Valley Cabernet Sauvignon sneaks into the mix—and part ownership of Viña Cobos in Argentina. "Argentina is sort of a utopia for frontiersmen. A rugged, independent spirit throbs vibrantly in every corner of the country. Plus, working here and in South America, I get two vintages a year to learn from!"

THE HOMMAGE LABELS

A vitally important part of the *Hommage* series is the art work, something of a paean to Chateau Mouton Rothschild, the first to incorporate modern art into the labeling of equally artistically-fashioned wines. "I remember being impressed when Mouton used a Picasso for the 1973 vintage,"

recalls Jan. "They used their own Picasso the year he died, since he had refused to do the customary drawing in exchange for wine while he was alive. It was also the year that Mouton was finally elevated to First Growth status. It seemed appropriate."

Shrem chose the French term 'Hommage' to designate his reserve wines as a means of offering tribute to the memory of the artist whose painting graces the label. "It is a tribute, too, to all of the people—the growers, the enologists, the artisans, the craftsmen, the workers—whose efforts are reflected in the wines we make here." Some of the recent artists selected include Oscar Dominguez, Paul Klee, Karel Appel's large, imposing, brightly colorful "Reclining Nude," Graham Sutherland's dark "Study of Foliage," and the jarring surrealistic

work of the Austrian Wolfgang Paalen.

Each year, Jan and Mitsuko select a different work, one for the Chardonnay, one for the Cabernet Sauvignon, from their expansive personal collection. "We are fortunate," says Jan in a clearly crafted 'off-the-cuff' remark. "Mitsuko and I own three hundred original paintings…so we have enough for the next hundred and fifty vintages of *Hommage*!"

Left: Hans Hartung (1904-1989) Lyrical Composition, 1948.

Right: Roberto Matta (1911-2002) Levitation in Blue, 1942.

THE WINEMAKER: SHAUN RICHARDSON

"There is a devil in every berry of the grape." – *The Koran*

Shaun Richardson was born in Melbourne, Australia on the sixth of September 1968. His mother was an administrative assistant in a restaurant, while his father was in marketing. "My parents drank a glass of wine with dinner every night," he says, "which seemed normal at the time, but in retrospect, it was certainly uncommon in the 70's". Developing a passion for food via family and friends in the restaurant industry, he took four years off after high school to explore cooking before returning to Roseworthy College (now Adelaide University) to direct his attentions to a Bachelors Degree in Enology. "I really liked cooking," says the affable lefty, "but as a chef, you lose your life every day. As a winemaker, you only lose your life—for the harvest—for two months out of the year. Of course, when our first child was born, my wife told me that I was going to have to try and balance my life, even during harvest!"

He was lucky at Roseworthy. "The year after I finished, enology became a four year program, more scientifically oriented, and less practically so, which was the reason Roseworthy had developed into one of the top five Enology programs

worldwide." Richardson is certainly a practical person, and if a thing can be done in three years, hey, why waste four? Of course, luck did not stop him graduating at the top of his class.

Like many of us, he remembers the first wine that really demanded his attention and nudged him to consider wine as a career. "It was a Pinot Noir from Yarra Burn, in the Yarra Valley. The intensity of the flavors made me take notice. There was a lot going on, and what it mostly did was make me want to know more. And then there were many Barossa Valley Shiraz wines that really solidified the decision. Those were—and are— wines of great intensity and individuality."

While still in school, he spent one crush each at Coriole Vineyards (known for Syrah, in McLaren Vale) and at Coldstream Hills (known for Pinot Noir and Chardonnay, in the Yarra Valley). "Coldstream was owned by the noted wine writer James Halliday. The great thing about working for James was that dinner for the crush crew was at his house each evening, and he would often bring out incredible French wines, many Burgundies (the grail of Pinot Noir), and many were utterly

Celebrating the start of harvest.

exquisite. From the moment I arrived I didn't realize what I was in for – Sunday dinner, my first day, was roasted pork complemented by a four-wine vertical of Alsatian Rieslings from Hugel, starting with 1945!"

His third crush job—he still hadn't worked through a full year at any stop at that point—was at Hardy's Wines, a much larger operation (nearly four million cases from one cellar). After a stint in retail sales to learn about customer service and brand development, he was ready to get back into production. "I really like the practical side of winemaking, digging out red pomace after fermentation, monitoring a wine's progress, running a pump, and I missed it in retail. I looked at the *Wine Spectator* 'Top 100' listing on their

web site, which in the late 90's was certainly more primitive than it is today, and picked out ten high-quality wineries that sounded interesting, and faxed my résumé out to them (email also being very primitive in 1997). Wine of the Year in 1996 was Beringer's Private Reserve Chardonnay – I applied there because I could have sworn the review made them sound like a tiny boutique winery! Naturally I applied to Geyser Peak, renowned in Australia for hiring Aussie interns every year, and for its Australian winemaker."

Richardson was snapped up by Saintsbury, so he had one more crush job, this for the harvest of 1997. When Saintsbury's winemaker Byron Kosuge recommended him to Steve Rogstad, then the Clos Pegase winemaker, Richardson was hired

Opposite: Beginning the Cabernet Sauvignon winemaking process with the careful selection of only perfect berries from the clusters.

Above: Cabernet Sauvignon from the Applebone Vineyard processed within hours of the harvest.

Many hands make light work of removing every speck of grape stem and leaf fragment before the grapes reach the tanks.

as enologist. A year later he was promoted to assistant winemaker; on the first of January 2002 he became head winemaker.

"Much as I enjoyed cooking, it didn't have the intellectual challenges that winemaking brings to the table. Winemaking is sensory food and brain food, combined." Richardson is fascinated by philosophy and cultural theory and recently waded his way through Jacques Derrida's *Of Grammatology.* "It's the most perplexing and confounding book I've ever read: I honestly can't

decide whether the man was a genius or a fraud".

One of the most fascinating parts of the winemaker's life is blending wines, the Bordeaux reds perhaps the pinnacle of that process. They've proven that for centuries in that corner of France, and we've known it here for better than a half century, starting with the efforts of the late Louis P. Martini.

Richardson gives a winemaking class at Napa Valley Junior College each year in March: "Over the years we've narrowed the focus of that class

to the red Bordeaux varieties, and it is fun to show the students what happens when distinctly different wines are blended to form something greater than the sum of the parts. I explain how, in Bordeaux, each region has different climate and soils, and that four hundred years of trial and error have allowed the Bordelaise to understand where each of the five varieties thrives. Cabernet Sauvignon excels in the Medoc and Haut-Medoc appellations on the Left Bank of the Gironde River, the great example being Chateau Latour. A

little south, in Graves, Cabernet Sauvignon is still king, but Merlot and Cabernet Franc are planted in large areas, Chateau Haut Brion being a good example. Merlot does especially well, as does Cabernet Franc, closer inland on the Right Bank in the appellations of Pomerol (Chateau Petrus) and St. Emilion (Chateau Cheval Blanc). The key is the *terroir* of the site, that unique combination of climate and soil. In each region, and specifically at each estate, the vineyard manager plants proportionally the blend of grapes that can

Cleanliness is the mantra of fine winemaking. About seven gallons of water are used in cleaning for every gallon of wine produced.

Above: Hand harvesting is used exclusively, and is one of many steps in the gentle handling and respect for each vineyard parcel.

Opposite: The rewards of dedication to fine wine and art.

consistently produce the greatest wine year-in and year-out. No estate is a hundred percent committed to one variety: even Petrus, the darling of the Merlot lovers, has five percent of its planting devoted to Cabernet Franc. Even so, the blend changes from year to year, depending on harvest quantity and quality." True there, true here.

That the Clos Pegase reds are so expressive is in large part due to Richardson's ability to recognize "flavor maturity" in the vineyards he oversees. This has been the single most important aspect in the vast improvement of wine quality in California over the last two decades. Before, grapes were picked on sugar content, with a goal of matching the classic French wines, without regard to the unique nature of the new world. Result? Wines that were not expressive of their site. Things only got better when winemakers began to pick based on flavor, although the past decade has seen wines of excessive ripeness, tasting of raisins and prunes. Richardson's focus on balance and elegance in wine has thankfully avoided this.

The charming thing about Richardson is that he connects so easily with people. Maybe it's

because he's an Aussie, or perhaps it's because he's a genuine fan of humanity. "What does 'perfectly ripe' mean?" he asks rhetorically. "Put a bunch of bananas on the counter and ask which one is perfectly ripe. Everyone will have a different opinion, based primarily on sight, but also on smell. None is right or wrong; they are correct for the person concerned."

Of course, unlike grapes, bananas continue to ripen after they are picked. The Richardsons have various fruit trees in their garden. "The first time we picked the pears—having patiently waited for perfect ripeness—we found that the fruit had rotted in the middle. We learned that you have to pick pears slightly green then let them ripen off the tree a week or so. But our figs are different, more like grapes: figs stop ripening the moment they are picked, so you really have to pay attention. That's why we (winemakers) spend so much time in the vineyard, looking at the health of the vines and tasting the berries to have the best sense possible of where the fruit is in terms of its flavor profile. However precisely we can measure sugar, acid, and tannins—and we can easily measure these—flavor is still the most important." Indeed, because that, in the final instance, is how we measure that quality of the wine. How does it taste?

78

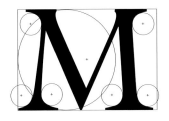

MITSUKO: THE ARTIST IN THE FAMILY

"A laborer works with his hands. A craftsman works with his hands and his brain.
An artist works with his hands, his brain and his heart." – *Old saying*

Every family should have someone with the artist's sensibilities lest life be reduced to the mundane, the practical, the ordinary. Trust me, there's nothing ordinary about Mitsuko Shinohara, born into an old samurai family in post-feudal, pre-World War II Tokyo.

"Those were difficult times," she says quietly. "My father was an Army officer, an administrator who never saw combat; he later lost his position. My mother wanted to be a doctor, but was allowed only to study midwifery, which she was never able to practice. My mother was a very strong person. If it could have been done, in that time and place, she would have done it."

Mitsuko has one sister and two brothers. "I wanted to study modern art, but my mother was against it. Early in my life, I was in a Christian mission school. Later, in college, I studied literature, both Japanese and English. Keats, Shelley and Yeats were my favorites. Yeats wrote about ghosts, and all I wanted to do was to talk with Irish people about ghosts! Much later, when I met the great chef Madeline Kaman, who ran the Great Chefs program at Beringer Vineyards for

years, she confided to me that she believed there were beneficial ghosts in the old Hudson House." Hudson House was the first home to the brothers Beringer; Jacob lived in the house, originally built in 1848, until his death in 1915. Hudson House— since marvelously restored—is now the site of Beringer Vineyards' Culinary Arts Center.

One great love of Mitsuko's life today is tennis, a game she approaches with an un-Japanese ferocity. "I love to play the net; most people like to smash the ball, not me; I like to surprise them and drop the ball." She laughs, with a merry light in her eyes. That attitude should be no surprise, in that she has great admiration for Andre Agassi and Pete Sampras. "We had lawn tennis when I was in high school; in the 50s; to flatten the lawn, we had to pull a giant roller which seemed to me to weigh almost as much as an elephant. Thank heaven for modern times. My father was a very good tennis player. I really learned to play with Jan when we were living in Paris."

"Some days I relish the opportunity to get out of the house! I just drive over to the public court in Calistoga. There's always someone ready to play.

No schedules; you just go."

Mitsuko is constantly on the go. In addition to having other homes in San Francisco and New York, she and Jan maintain an intense travel schedule, both for work and for pleasure. Among her many talents, she is a truly creative landscape designer, evidenced in the winery grounds. "I am very interested in plants, and how they grow. I plan to study bonsai on our next trip to Japan. The arrangement of plants and flowers appeals to my artistic side. I like to make something." The dining room of their home overlooks the pool and garden, a garden that clearly shows Mitsuko's tasteful, understated approach to landscape design.

She recently designed and patented a unique tennis visor and is working on a mesh-like tennis shirt that would help players stay cool on the court. Mitsuko is very creative, but not on the business side of things. "We were ready to go into production on the visor, but producing five hundred did not interest the manufacturers...and ten thousand was just too many! There wasn't much to be done in that vast middle ground. The labor is always the costliest part of any such product, and we wanted to be able to avoid the salesmen and do our selling on the internet. We'll see how it plays out."

Typical of the artistic temperament, Mitsuko also knows her way around the kitchen. "Part of the reason I retired was to spend more time in the kitchen," she says, then turns around a hundred eighty degrees, with her wickedly ironic sense of humor, to add, "I'm a perfectionist, so now, with the children grown, we eat out mostly!"

Not true. "Actually, I was a borderline diabetic and, all of a sudden, I had to pay very close attention to what I was eating. So we are very careful about our diet, very health conscious. I pay very close attention to the ingredients I use. We entertained a lot when we lived in Paris, and game was a big part of our cuisine there. Now, we eat a lot of vegetables, often with lamb. Still, Japanese cuisine has had a very deep influence, in particular on Western cooking in general. You see it especially in the last thirty years, with the Japanese respect for the character of raw materials, light cooking, and minimalist presentation. Japanese techniques have equally influenced today's taste, advancing the popularity of Japanese foods, like sushi. We particularly like grilled fish, without oil, and seasoned lightly with salt only, served with steamed vegetables."

"I often use tofu, which can be very tasty when you make use of salt, lemon juice and olive oil to give it additional texture and flavor. You add chives to cubed tofu, and it goes very nicely with wine. You'd be surprised! We do eat out a lot. Locally, we are very fond of Thomas Keller (proprietor of the famed French Laundry, in nearby Yountville), though we're just as likely to entertain friends at the excellent oriental restaurant right here in Calistoga."

Mitsuko stops to mention that she once prepared her favorite tofu dish for Thomas Keller: "Uncooked cubes, remember, with just a few drops of olive oil, a dash of salt, and chives on top. He was still praising this dish ten years later!" she says exultantly, "and if you pass on the 'usual' soy sauce, it goes far better with wine."

The Shrems have two sons. "David, the older, is a free spirit," she says. "He has a business with friends in San Francisco, and is quite a good cook.

The Winter Garden at the Shrems' residence.

Marc, a year younger, lives in Los Angeles and has a passion for acting. He was an honors student and loves to read. He has spent more than a dozen years pursuing a career in acting, but so far, only got small parts."

Gail Gordon has known Mitsuko more than thirty years. A Chicago native and a working artist in her own right: she composes music on the one hand, and is involved in the use of refracted light on the other. "I really liked her, right off the bat. She's a devout friend, and a person that lights up a room!" Gail and her husband Roy, an

Above: Mitsuko's artistic creation at the entrance to Clos Pegase: Two Spheres: one small on a tall pedestal, one large on a short pedestal (the former shown here).

Opposite: Mitsuko and Jan in the Reserve Tasting Room flanked by works from Herbin (left) and Matta (right).

internationally-known aqua culturist, a pioneer in land-based fish-farming, have traveled with the Shrems or hosted them at their coast-side Bodega Bay home. "It's not so much any specific thing we do, we just enjoy being together. We are interested and excited about everything and we have such great conversations. I love to see the playfulness that Jan and Mitsuko have together and she simply brings a smile and warmth to everything she touches. She is a very charismatic woman."

Mitsuko is herself an avid reader, and

appreciates Harry Truman's maxim that "The only thing new in the world is the history you haven't read." "That's true, I particularly love to read history," she says. "I read a lot of newspapers, particularly the New York Times. I just finished reading William Glasser's book, Choice Theory. It's about understanding the mathematical nature of how we make decisions in our lives."

As to music, Mitsuko falls back on the artist's eclecticism to say that she is utterly and completely devoted to classical music…and Elvis Presley. "I

love Mozart and Wagner, but I also am taken with Elvis. He had such a cute face, but it was so sad to see such a talent in so self-destructive a person, but there you are. His voice was unique. Jan is a big opera buff—he likes Wagner, Handel, Gluck—but he's also graduated to Philip Glass, too. 'Nixon in China' is one of his favorites. We were recently at a San Francisco Opera production of 'Don Giovanni.' It was extraordinary, magnificent!"

As you might imagine, the influence of Japanese art has and continues to play a great part in her life. "There is no change between then and now. Japanese art and tradition is the deepest root of my life and my artistic sensibilities; it always stays in my entire consciousness. Of course, living in the modern world, and traveling as much as we do, it also contributes to my sense of taste. But remember, Japanese art has always had a lot of influence on international art—and has given much to architecture as well as the culinary world—and that has continued to this day. Also, Japanese artisans have also given much to the world, particularly in their close attention to detail and to presentation."

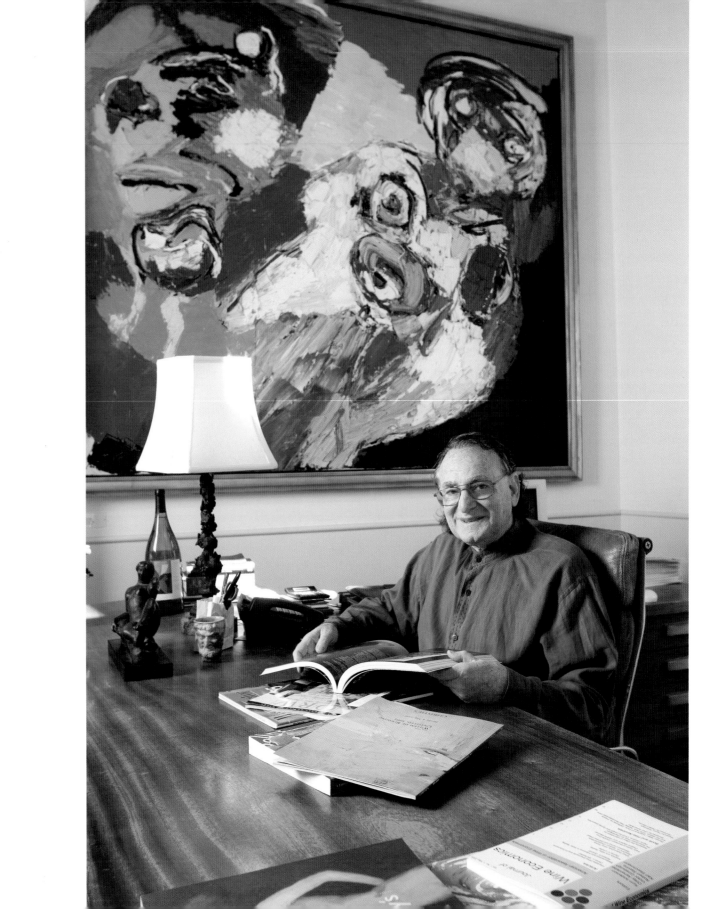

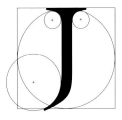

JAN SHREM: ARTISTIC EXPRESSION

"To be what we are and to become what we are capable of becoming, is the only end in life."
–Dutch philosopher Baruch Spinoza, 1632-1677

The wooden floor of his office—and its simple, flat desk—betray little of the man, other than, perhaps, a sense of simple elegance, a sense of unvarnished purity. It is when you take in the near Spartan artistic embellishments that you begin to see the intelligence and artistic vision that drives the man.

From his early days, selling encyclopedias door-to-door, to the present day success of his well-thought-out vineyard and winery, Jan Shrem has demonstrated a single-mindedness of purpose that has forded streams, brooked challenges and surmounted setbacks. "Determination" turns out to be a pale descriptor. Nietzsche's "will-to-power" might be more like it.

Shrem could be dubbed "multifacetic": a man of many facets. It is a quality endemic to the wine business, primarily because wine is necessarily a business that routinely draws upon many and diverse talents and resources. The waters quickly run shallow with most folks once you get past their immediate area of expertise. Not so with winegrowers, who must know something of agriculture, science, religion, technology,

architecture, art, business, marketing…and put an intuitive twist on all of the above if he or she is to fly high into the sky.

Shrem offers as good an example of the multifacetic winegrower as exists in an era when words like "multi-tasking" and "cross-training" are easily tossed off but rarely truly understood and valued. Nearing 80, he has the energy and curiosity of a fairly vital fellow a third his age. A one-time publisher—in Japan where he met Mitsuko, in France where he came to appreciate artistically envisioned wines—he evolved once to art, and thence to wine in fleshing out his enchantingly, philosophically multi-articulated *curriculum vitae*.

Jan was born to Jewish-Lebanese parents in Colombia, South America in 1930. He was just two when the family moved to Jerusalem. "My father, Joseph, was a traveling salesman. Descended from a long line of rabbis, he was not an academic at all. He met my mother on the day they were married— it was an arranged marriage—and it did not go well. Born in Beirut but raised in Egypt, my mother played the violin and the piano, and spoke French.

Karel Appel's (1921-2006)
Lying Nude, 1966, majestically
oversees Jan's desk.

Robert Mondavi, Margrit Biever Mondavi, Edward Schmidt, Jan Shrem, and Michael Graves with the winning architectural design.

Her father was a tailor, but an enlightened man."

Joseph had moved the family to South America at the outset of the Depression, in hopes of finding work. In 1932 his wife Rose returned to the Middle East, settling in Jerusalem with Jan and his two siblings. "When Mitsuko and I visited Jerusalem a few years ago, the stone house we lived in was still standing! In 1939 mother took us back to our father in Colombia, where I lived until 1946, when an

aunt living in New York helped me to get there. I came on a freight plane. I was the only passenger! I lived in the YMCA, first a messenger boy and then a typist and went to high school at night."

Shrem attributes his perseverance and his will to succeed to his Jewish heritage. "Remember, the men were obligated to read the Bible—from beginning to end—at least once a year. They had to learn to read *long before Christ*. That academic tradition, I think, created both the will to survive and the means to survive. You have to remember that I worked my way through college—for five solid years— selling encyclopedias door-to-door. I cannot count how many times I would go to twenty or thirty homes, take 'no' for an answer, and then be invited in for a piece of pie, a cup of coffee… and a sale. I was a very good salesman. Very good." How good? "Very good. I drove a Cadillac!"

Shrem earned his Bachelor's degree in political science at the University of Utah, then moved on to UCLA to begin his Master's in international law. "At that time, I wanted to go to work for the United Nations, do something in the international field. Then a Japanese young lady I was going with talked me into going to Japan for a visit." That off-the-cuff two-week visit to Japan…turned into a thirteen-year stay. "I was completely fascinated by a country that was still anchored in feudal customs," he remembers in wonder. "It reminded me, in many ways, of my own youth, raised in an orthodox culture that was founded on respect for elders and for knowledge."

"It was, of course—as a foreigner, as a *gaijin*—impossible for me to find employment in Japan, so I was forced to start my own business. From selling encyclopedias I had developed a passion for books; I knew these were indispensable in Japan. At that time there, publishing was a most promising and undeveloped field. Nothing at all existed in the way of foreign technical and scientific volumes. Oh, there were a few archaic tomes, and some in the German language, in that German had been the dominant scientific language through World War II."

Shrem's vision of importing and introducing millions of fundamental works—in English—became the standard references in those rather specialized domains. When he sold the business 13 years later he had 2,000 Japanese employees, and he had built several new office structures—having once dreamed of becoming an architect, he reveled in the opportunity—which supported his rapidly-growing, wildly-successful business. That, in turn, further piqued his burgeoning interest in the art world, so much so that he opened an art gallery. The wheels of fate were turning. Rapidly.

One of the employees in his Tokyo art gallery—he called it Kiriko, after the great artist, the Italian master of surrealism, Giorgio de Chirico—was a young Japanese ceramist and art student by the name of Mitsuko, soon to become wife and partner. "My love of art was, then, still a little raw," Jan confesses. "Though I had painted as a child, and had an eye for ancient art, Mitsuko really had an artist's 'eye' for quality. I soon managed to recognize her talent, and from that moment on we always did our buying of art together, with a common accord, a shared appreciation."

In 1968 Jan sold his Japanese businesses and left for Europe with Mitsuko, living in London for a short time before settling in Milan. Jan joined the Fabbri publishing company, where his focus was on producing elegantly illustrated art books. "We have always loved to travel," he recalls, "and we would visit the great European and American art exhibits, like the Biennale in Venice and the Documenta in Cassel, Germany. As we became familiar with contemporary artists, we began to buy and collect. With a passion, yes, and I think a bit of perspicacity."

"We were not afraid to go out of our way to meet a new artist," adds Mitsuko, "and we were happy to examine a hundred works just to select one. Some will purchase many works of an artist, but we were looking for the best of the best, the works that truly represented the artist in his or her best period. We didn't want to fall into the trap of 'love at first sight.' Too emotional. We wanted those works that would stand the test of time, works that create tension and were complex enough to bring you back, time after time, pieces that would continue to be interesting and challenge the viewer years and decades later."

After two years in Milan, it was the 'City of Lights.' "We felt that Paris would be better, in terms of upbringing, for our children," says Mitsuko. "Paris is a very livable city. We moved into a beautiful four-floor house that was part of the Parc de Montretout in Saint Cloud, where Napoleon built some villas for his marshals, directly across the Seine River and Bois de Boulogne, overlooking all Paris. One of our neighbors was the actor Lino Ventura (Italian-born, best known for parts in *The Three Penny Opera* and *The Valachi Papers*)." The stables had been converted into a garage as well as guest quarters, which Mitsuko converted into her pottery studio, and Jan begun gardening for the first time (not successfully).

Though Paris was supposedly Jan's retirement-at-fifty, it didn't quite turn out that way. "Mitsuko would tell me, 'I married you for better or for worse, but not for *lunch*—go back to work!'" Even the maid complained that Jan was home all the time, supposedly writing a book on the adventure of modern art, which Mitsuko did not think much of.

Jan quietly credits Mitsuko with inculcating his interest in wine: "I was thirty when I met Mitsuko and, curiously, it was she who lured me to my life-long love of wine. To this day, she still claims a small royalty on the bottle we share each evening. When we were living in Paris, our friendship with Eric de Rothschild nudged my interest along to a different plane entirely. A connoisseur of both art and wine, Eric—who later took over the reins of Chateau Lafite Rothschild—became a business partner as well. We owned a company together, as

Jan Shrem in the cellar at Clos Pegase (c. 1987).

The entrance portico, with Henry Moore's 'Mother Earth.'

an investment," says Shrem with a rueful laugh. "I think we each lost about a million dollars on that one!"

Twenty-five years as a publisher was enough. "I sold the business to pursue my passion for wine," he says with a sly smile. "I was so intent upon doing it right, that I undertook studies at the University of Bordeaux. Since then, I have been initiated into the mysteries and art of growing grapes and making wine, and learned to look for the elusive aromas of, say, violet and blackberry

and raspberry in the Cabernet. *Wine has become the great adventure in my life."* An understatement nearly British in magnitude.

Returning to the States, Jan spent nearly three years searching for the right place to begin a project that would combine his interests in art, architecture and wine. It was, clearly, this multi-faceted nature of wine—drawing equally from agriculture and science, intuition and the empirical—that drew him inexorably to wine. He came to California because that was where all the exciting enological breakthroughs were happening, at such a remarkable pace that French and Italian producers were sending their children there, to attend Davis or Fresno, to do internships at Golden State wineries. "When it became obvious to me that Napa was the Bordeaux of America—poised to rise in greatness and international renown—we knew that we had found the place. I found a magical place in an enchanted valley." What more could one ask for, short of being greedy?

Shrem has served on the board of the International Sculpture Center and has been a member of the Director's Circle of the San

Francisco Museum of Modern Art. He has also been proud to serve the Family Winemakers of California, chaired charity wine and art auctions for schools and museums and hosted or contributed to hundreds of fund raisers for museums, universities and wine societies, often offering his humor-laden, leaning-towards-the-sensual slide lecture 'Bacchus the Rascal: Four Thousand Years of Wine in Art.'

Travel is one of the Shrems great loves. "Happiness, for me, consists of many small pleasures, frequently repeated. A glass of wine in your favorite armchair; a good meal with friends and partners. Mitsuko and I take great pleasure in travel. Travel is enriching, especially when you combine it with art, history and architecture. And I get to read more when I am traveling than at home."

He extemporizes on a week-long trip he and Mitsuko took with the directors of San Francisco's Museum of Modern Art: "We were in Istanbul and Venice to view the art *biennales* in both cities. The one in Venice has been showcasing the best in contemporary art from many nations for over a century; Istanbul's is a beginner, but still has merit. We also enjoyed the Hippodrome, the Topkapi Palace, the Blue Mosque, the St. Savior Church, the great Byzantine mosaics and frescoes, the Archaeological Museum, the Hagia Sophia Church and Emperor Justinian's vaulted cistern—it has three hundred thirty-three marble columns—taken from the Greek and Roman pagan temples, where you literally can *walk on water.*" They arose at five in the morning on one day, in Venice, to take the special tour to Padua to see Giotto's recently restored 13th century Scrovengi Chapel.

Jan and Mitsuko regularly host wine-and-art cruises for their 5,000 member wine club, the Pegase Circle. On Crystal Cruises they sailed from Buenos Aires to Chile (through the Antarctic), and from Copenhagen to the Norway fjords to the Artic and back to England. One excursion featured a river cruise down the Danube, while another on the Rhone River in Burgundy. They do have fun, these folks.

As his "My Club" groups of friends well know, Jan avidly employs the internet to share items of bawdy humor, inventive artistic flair (three-

A toast to the Napa Valley.

dimensional sidewalk art so realistic that you fear falling into a stairwell that isn't there), simple joy (sometimes schmaltzy, always satisfying), and lasting philosophical wisdom. One posting—in the last category—was of Dr. Randy Pausch's "Last Lecture" at Carnegie-Mellon University. It is a tradition there that special professors are asked to give a lecture summing up their life-acquired wisdom as if it embodied the last words they might speak in their lives.

As it happened for Pausch—he had pancreatic cancer—it was his last, but he admonished his audience to take the same life-affirming approach he took. He talked about how his parents were so open to life that they allowed him, as a teen, to paint anything he wanted on his bedroom wall (a fake elevator door and the quadratic equation). He told how he poured a can of soda on the back seat of his new convertible while his nephew and niece's mother was telling them to be extra careful in the new car. "It's just a *thing*," he told his sister. "I don't want my nephew to feel guilty if he has to throw up in my car if he has the flu." Pausch suggested that his listeners be Tigger and not

Eeyore, and retain the bounce and the spirit, if not the facts as well, of their childhood dreams. "Brick walls are there for a reason, to let us prove how badly we want things. You can't change the hand you're dealt in life, but you can choose how you *play* it." More than anything else he said, "When you've wronged someone, tell them you're sorry, admit that the fault was yours, and—this is the least done/most important part—ask them how you can make things right."

Joel Barrish M.D. is a close family friend. "I lived in New York for ten years, just a few blocks away from where Jan and Mitsuko have an apartment, and we'd spend time together going to auctions, art galleries and museums," says the academic internist. "When I retired, I spent a year teaching in Tokyo, and we'd meet and do the same thing when the Shrems were in Japan for the month of December each year. I'm not much of a wine nut, but Jan has taught me so much that I can no longer get away with the cheap stuff, darn it! Mitsuko keeps a room for me in Calistoga almost like it was my home away from home. I love Jan's quirky *joie de vivre* and Mitsuko's wry

94

sense of humor. When Jan is traveling and Mitsuko is in their San Francisco apartment, I'll take her shopping or to dinner to make sure she's doing okay. An evening with the Shrems is always delightful, eclectic and enlightening. When I had to undergo surgery awhile back, they hovered, deeply concerned about my well-being. They are kind, caring and generous."

Another good friend is urologist Marc Cohen, a Philadelphia native who has known Jan for more than two decades. "Jan has this odd eccentricity, in that he easily donates large sums of money to causes he believes in, is happy to pay value for value in the worlds of art and wine... yet he'll take a bus before a taxi or drive around the block four times rather than pay for parking! He has a computer-like brain, coupled with a native brilliance when it comes to marketing and sales; I've never met so successful a salesman *who was also honest.*"

Cohen points to an inherent modesty, a shyness that allows Shrem to easily give credit to those who work for him, and to Jan's enduring love for Mitsuko. "I remember inviting Jan to a boys'

dinner when Mitsuko was going to San Francisco for a girls' night out. During our dinner, Jan kept going outside to phone Mitsuko until he finally reached her and was satisfied that everything was okay. I admire that his mental and physical strength, his humility, loyalty and integrity have never faltered, no matter what challenges were happening in his life." (Interestingly, Cohen has become so entranced by the wine business that he's started his own small winery, Howell at the Moon, with Jan his mentor.)

What I like most about Jan is his adamant and continuing zest for new experience, be it in art or wine or that broadest of categories, general knowledge. The "educated Jewish survivor" that he talks about is alive and well, bawdy and witty, and residing in Calistoga...and in many other parts of this fascinating orb. A man who is truly becoming everything that he is capable of becoming, Jan is a true citizen of the world he is so thoroughly amused by and immersed in.

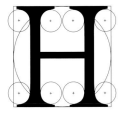 HUMOR, ART, HISTORY, HEALTH & RELIGION

"A man cannot make him laugh; but that's no marvel, he drinks no wine." – *William Shakespeare*

"A man without mirth is like a wagon without springs. He is jolted disagreeably by every pebble in the road." – *Henry Ward Beecher*

Humor may be the one thing that most sets us apart from other animals, notwithstanding the plethora of staged pictures purporting to demonstrate animal mirth. As the great Dane, pianist-comic Victor Borge once noted, "Laughter is the shortest distance between two people."

Jan understands that concept implicitly, and humor has always been a key ingredient in the Shrem arsenal. Members of his e-mail "My Club" know that his funny bone has exhaustive range, from the downright silly to the utterly sublime, from the raw and scatological to the wryly religious. Jan has an equally impish and bawdy-to-the-point-of-lusty side as well, which makes for some utterly delightful submissions to his Club. Avidly a-religious, he nonetheless reminds one and all of the vast cultural contribution those of the Jewish heritage have proffered over the millennia.

And, of course, Jan and the winery used to host the "Grapes of Laugh," a series of humor competitions themed but not restricted to wine-related jokes and amusing stories, including a story attributed to the renowned wine writer Bob Thompson about a Frenchman dining in a country bistro, his faithful pooch by his side. When the wine waiter came to take the man's beverage order, the doughty Frenchman said, "A glass of Volnay for me, I think, and a little Beaune for my *chien*!" Another great contribution to the "Grapes of Laugh" had to do with a local winemaker, whose wines were not of the highest quality, pestering a New York wine writer to cover his wines. When, one day, the winemaker discovered the writer taking lunch at a local restaurant, he hustled to his cellar to bring some samples to the writer's table. Unable to graciously put off the persistent winemaker, the writer gamely tried the wines, wincing at their obvious flaws. Finally, when the winemaker absolutely insisted upon a response, the writer muttered, "Don't travel well, do they."

Elyn Zimmerman (b. 1945)
Palisades Project, 1981
(foreground).

Anthony Caro (b. 1924)
Sunshine, 1964 (background).

The working winery is filled with an eclectic mix of art, such as Alternative View of Mastaba, 1967 by Robert Grosvenor (b. 1937) in the extreme right front, and historical viticultural tools on the wall.

ART AND HISTORY

It was in Paris that Jan and Mitsuko began to weave ties to the creative community, ties that would lead in one direction to an incredible art collection, and in another to Jan's Napa Valley temple of wine, Clos Pegase. "We frequented artists' studios, we visited galleries," says Jan. "I think that's why our collection has so wide a range, such vitality. We started out focusing on the Surrealists, like Salvador Dali, Francis Picabia and Max Ernst. We were also taken with the Danish-influenced CoBrA school, which included such artists as Pierre Alechinsky, Karel Appel, Corneille and Constant. But we couldn't neglect the French, so we were also collecting Jean Dubuffet, Pierre Soulages and César. We became good friends with the Latin American painter Fernando Botero, and bought his paintings. We loved the auction houses, which we attended with like-minded friends, but we all agreed that we wouldn't bid against each

other so as not to put stress on our friendships. Sometimes we actually drew lots to determine who would be allowed to bid on a particular painting!"

Later, when they had moved to California, the Shrems' interests turned toward Minimalists like Robert Ryman. Outdoor sculpture is a big deal at Clos Pegase. The gardens are almost magical with the works of Dubuffet, Henry Moore, Mark di Suvero, Louise Bourgeois, Robert Morris, Richard Serra and Tony Cragg.

In the tasting rooms, there are tasting vessels that go back four millennia, pieces from Syria, the Roman Empire, China, Korea and Japan. "It's funny, but we began collecting these pieces well before we thought of growing grapes and making wine," says Jan, raising his most expressive eyebrows.

Shrem takes great pleasure showing guests through the winery and its grounds. He also has an extraordinary presentation entitled "Bacchus

the Rascal: A Bacchanalian History of Wine Seen Through 4,000 Years of Art." Shrem has given this witty, humorous and informative perambulation hundreds of times—often to charitable purpose—at universities, museums, wine and food societies, and art and educational foundations from Pacific to Atlantic. "It is important that people see the connection between wine and art, and that they understand that the moderate application of wine to their daily lives is conducive to a healthier and more graceful way of life." Spanning vinous art from artists at Antioch and Persepolis (2000 B.C.) to Leonardo da Vinci ("Bacchus," which hangs in the Louvre), Shrem's tour de force was "appreciated so much by the Commonwealth Club in San Francisco, among others, that they invited me to repeat it three more times!" After a showing at Boston University's School of Medicine, Dr. Curtis Ellison—he does cutting edge research on the health benefits of wine, and was interviewed twice on the subject by *60 Minutes*—wrote Jan: "I have had dozens of people tell me how informative and enjoyable it was. I think that the points you

bring out in your presentation help set an historical basis for much of our research. Your presentation and your wines played a major part in making the celebration a success…"

"It helps to remember," adds Shrem, "that Dionysus was not a myth to the Greeks, but a very palpable fact. To drink wine meant to have the god of wine inside you, easing the cares of the day. Wine was also the drink that helped nurture civilization in Greece and the Aegean. Religious ceremonies in honor of Dionysus brought coherent organization to music and dance and gave birth to the theater. It is little wonder, then, that the vine and its fruits appear in every artistic movement of note."

ART AND THE WINE LABEL

Wine labels have long provided an avenue of expression for winegrowers like Jan Shrem. Most known are the contemporary works—the art traded for cases of the wine—displayed on the labels of Chateau Mouton-Rothschild. From Picasso to the

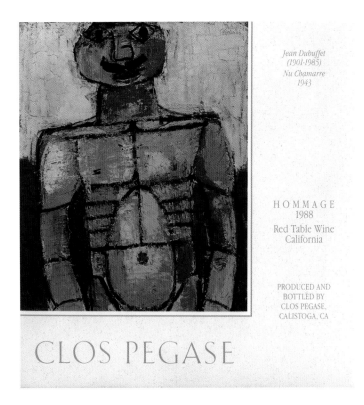

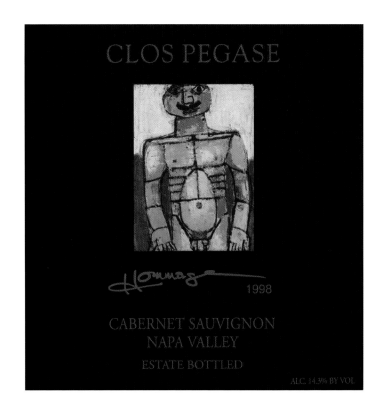

Jean Dubuffet (1901-1985) Nu Chamarre, 1943 in its censored form for the 1988 Hommage wine, and revealed as the "Full Monty" for the 1998 vintage.

Italian sculptor Giuseppe Penone, Mouton has set the standard for others to emulate.

As is always the case, there are the occasional setbacks when dealing with bureaucracy, most notably the two "nude" labels of Kenwood and Clos Pegase. Kenwood's very first artist series label in 1978 for the winery's 1975 Reserve Cabernet Sauvignon—poster artist David Lance Goines' "Naked Lady", a gracefully reclining nude on a vine-studded hillside—was rejected by the District of Columbia desk-sitters as "obscene and indecent." A second attempt—a brilliantly tongue-in-cheek reclining skeleton—was also rejected. The label that was finally accepted was the same scene minus the young lady; but, given the extensive press coverage given the prior attempts, everyone mentally replaced the lady on the slope.

Don't you know it, but Jan Shrem had a similar experience with the federal desk jockeys. When he presented them with the work of French painter Jean Dubuffet for his 1988 Hommage—the painting, *"Nu Chamarre"* (Bedecked Nude), features a subtle frontal nude male trunk—the label was summarily rejected. "When we cropped the painting—it is one of my favorites—to eliminate the genitals, I tried to include a note on the side label that said, 'For compliance requirements, part of this painting has required disguising,'" says Shrem with a rueful grin. "They rejected that as well. We only had two thousand cases of the wine and, with estimated court costs at forty thousand dollars, at that point it was no longer worth fighting even though we figured our chances of winning in court at ninety percent. One irony in all of this is that

Anthony Caro (b. 1924) Sunshine, 1964. After gaining a degree in Engineering and spending time as an assistant to Henry Moore in the 1950's, Caro moved to Vermont, where the sunny atmosphere helped create this piece.

Dubuffet was, for half his life…a wine merchant!" The further irony was that, a few years later, the feds recanted and allowed the label as originally proposed. Persistence is everything.

One of the reasons the bureaucrats gave for turning down the label was that Dubuffet was *not* an Old Master. "I'm not exactly sure of what that means," says Shrem. "Would I have to go back to Rembrandt? Michelangelo? Dubuffet was one of the most original and most uncompromising of post-war artists. The richness and versatility of his work is astonishing. He coined the term '*art brut*' to denote the spontaneous, unconscious and anti-conventional quality of his own style. Prices of Dubuffet works at auction were among the highest of post-war artists, frequently in the seven-digit range. I just assumed that he was Old Master enough. Beyond even that, it is extremely discouraging to see First Amendment rights infringed upon in a country that purports to support freedom of expression. Especially when our right to explain, for example, the proven health benefits of wine on our labels is equally *verboten*. That smacks of censorship, plain and simple."

Shrem is not beyond noting the intimate connections between wine and sensuality: "Casanova was a lover of the red grape, finding that it enhanced sexual pleasure. It turns out that there is a physiological link between the sense of smell and our genital organs, the aromatic compound in wine, pheromone. Interestingly, too, university studies have shown that a moderate intake of alcohol by women enhanced sexual arousal, but excessive intake has the opposite effect. With men? Even the *thought* of consumption was sufficient to induce arousal!"

WINE AND HEALTH

Curiously, health ought to be one of the most accessible arguments to spreading the culture of wine in this country. Virtually all that we know and continue to learn is on the plus side. As

Richard Deacon (b.1949) Smile, 1992. Preferring to be called a 'fabricator' rather than a 'sculptor,' his materials of choice invariably have structural potential.

pundits have noted, we have few food warning labels—despite the fact that obesity and heart problems lead the list for untimely death—and plenty of wine/alcohol warnings even though we know that a glass or two with dinner cuts heart and circulatory risk *by half*!

Some years ago the folks at Robert Mondavi Winery took the lead in this fight by promoting their "Mission" statement in support of wine as

a beverage of health (and a counter to a then-budding neo-prohibitionist sentiment). "Wine has been with us since the beginning of civilization," noted William Craig, a Mondavi educator. "It is the temperate, civilized, sacred, romantic mealtime beverage recommended in the Bible. Wine has been praised for centuries by statesmen, scholars, poets and philosophers…Wine stimulates not only the body but the mind." However, permission to print

this on a bottle was denied. Yet, as has been noted so often, the Italians consume up to ten times the amount of wine per person that Americans do, yet have one of the lowest rates of alcoholism and heart disease in the world. The Mediterranean diet—fish, fresh fruits and vegetables, plenty of pasta, a glass or two of the *vino*—has proven itself heart smart and effective for millennia.

No less than a spokesman for the Public Health Service has pointed out that the moderate use of wine improves digestion and helps us to more effectively absorb nutrients from food, which is vital to those, particularly geriatrics, who have a hard time getting all the nutrition they need. And we all know that a glass with dinner is a boon to those who find slumber difficult. A little of the red is beneficial when the head hits the pillow.

AND THEN THERE'S RELIGION

Though rarely talked-about, religion has always and forever played an important role in the spread and development of the culture of the vine. From the miracle of Cana—where Christ changed water into wine—to the continuing use of wine at a

wide variety of rites, wine has been central to the celebration and expansion of our spiritual lives. Consider further the "water into wine" metaphor. This is exactly what a grape vine does, season in and season out: it takes in water, works it with photosynthesis, and transforms it into a higher form of liquid.

It is a continuing curiosity that some will point to scripture to support a stand *against* the consumption of wine. Wine is mentioned innumerable times—several *hundred* times, in fact—in the Bible and, while one is often counseled against over-imbibing and against drinking a wine when it has yet to be properly aged, the wisely tempered use of wine is indeed championed by the good book.

See, as example, Proverbs 23:20: "Do not join those who drink too much wine or gorge themselves on meat." Then there are the frequent mentions of "wine and other fermented drink" (i.e. beer), which lays lie to those who suggest that "wine" in the Bible refers to unfermented grape juice. And references to "new wine" clearly have to do with aging wine properly and not allowing it

Jean Dubuffet (1901-1985)
Faribolus, 1973.

103

to spoil and turn to vinegar, a common problem in those days.

The admonition in First Timothy (5:23)—this is Paul, the great moralist, giving advice to the pastor Timothy—is perhaps the most quoted of all: "And use a little wine for thy stomach's sake and thine often infirmities." Seems that the ancient ones intuitively recognized the innate health benefits of wine—we know that it reduces heart and circulatory risk by *fifty percent* (hardly to be sneezed at)—not to mention wine's many social and spiritual benefits. In a nutshell, a glass or two with a meal is good for the heart, improves one's conversational input, brings out the fullest flavors of the food, and aids in its subsequent digestion. Without being greedy, what more could one reasonably request from this beneficent beverage? Or, to return to one authority (Psalms 104:15): "Wine that gladdens the heart of man, oil to make his face shine, and bread that sustains his heart." The *Talmud* is not lacking either: "Wine nourishes, refreshes and cheers. Wine is the foremost of all medicines." A positive approach.

Dr. M. Sheldon and J. McDonald, writing in *The American Journal of Clinical Nutrition*, sum things up for us rather nicely: "Wine is one of the oldest beverages known to man. Written records dating back 4,000 years refer to the dietary and therapeutic uses of wine. It has been attractive to man as food, as a medicine, as a part of various religious and ritual ceremonies throughout the world, and as an important element in social life. In light of its ancient history, it is not surprising that many of the healthful effects of wine have become legendary." Not a bad word, that.

Let us leave the last word to Mr. Shrem: "Wine is a mild, delicious intoxicant, and a potent vehicle of pleasure. It is also an ancient symbol for life, fertility and for cultural sophistication. The simple pleasures derived from a glass of wine become richer and more complex the greater one's knowledge of our shared past. Wine remains, as it has for millennia, a part of our diet that brings pleasure and a feeling of well-being and, more, serves as a living link to civilizations that have gone before."

104

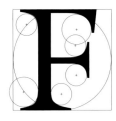

FINISH

"We do not see things as they are. We see things as we are."–*Talmud*

The greatest thing about wine is that it is such a cross-cultural marvel, drawing from talents and disciplines as varied as art and science, the intuitive and the religious and the agricultural and the business-like. It is a venture that brings out the very best in humankind, because each glass of wine reflects—rather accurately, if truth be told (and wine assures us that truth will be told)—the personalities of those involved in its naissance. The best of those personalities, like the best of their wines, have lingering essences—finish, in the lingo of wine—that inform; that stay with you.

So there is no surprise at all in learning that the winery and the wines of Jan and Mitsuko Shrem possess pizzazz and personality aplenty, that rare mix of uniqueness and flair, that marvelous mix of the eclectic and the constant that make for vitality and distinctiveness. In the sense that pets often take on the mannerisms of their owners, the wines of Clos Pegase are naturally expressive of the proprietors.

For all the hours that I have spent with these two extraordinary people in preparation for this book—walking their cellar, tasting their wines,

sharing their love of great art, conversation, literature, food and wine—one moment stands out in my mind as being definitive of their approach to their life lived in-and-amongst that wonderful world. We were in a hospitality suite, preparing to sit down to a light lunch after having tasted through the current releases and chatting about how they had met and how their lives had turned first to art, and thence to wine.

Jan and Mitsuko were sitting next to each other on a divan, and we were sharing observations about our children and about our tennis games (mine and Mitsuko's). As they sat there, certain long-married signals drew an almost teenage nudge here, a lighthearted giggle there. It was such a sweet and charming intimacy between two people who are so at home with one another, so comfortable in their places in the world—together or apart, but most especially together. To see things as these two see them, that would be a good thing.

Jan and Mitsuko show great pride in their 25 years of work creating Clos Pegase.

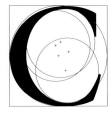

CREDITS

All photography by Faith Echtermeyer except as listed.

CLOS PEGASE WINERY
1060 Dunaweal Lane
Calistoga, California 94515

707-942-4981

email: tenma@clospegase.com

www.clospegase.com